Rick Steves

SNAPSHOT

Basque Country

Spain & France

CONTENTS

INTRODUCTION

This Snapshot guide, excerpted from my guidebook on Spain, introduces you to the Basque Country. This is the land where Spain and France meet the Atlantic—filled with people who have their own culture and language, but not their own country. Even without political independence, the Basque culture thrives in both countries. Here you can enjoy the cushy beach resorts of San Sebastián and Biarritz, just as European royalty did a hundred years ago. Or make a pilgrimage to the historic town of Guernica, where horrific bombing during the Spanish Civil War inspired a Picasso masterpiece. Visit Bilbao and Frank Gehry's dazzling temple of modern art—the Guggenheim Bilbao. Run with (or cheer on) the bulls in Pamplona. Linger in Bayonne, with its lively old town and impressive Museum of Basque Culture, and then head for the mellow port town of St-Jean-de-Luz. On both sides of the border, you'll see why the independent Basques have clung tightly to their heritage.

To help you have the best trip possible, I've included the following topics in this book:

• **Planning Your Time,** with advice on how to make the most of your limited time

• **Orientation,** including tourist information (abbreviated as TI), tips on public transportation, local tour options, and helpful hints

• **Sights** with ratings:

      ▲▲▲—Don't miss

      ▲▲—Try hard to see

      ▲—Worthwhile if you can make it

      No rating—Worth knowing about

• **Sleeping** and **Eating,** with good-value recommendations in every price range

- **Connections,** with tips on trains, buses, and driving

Practicalities, near the end of this book, has information on money, phoning, hotel reservations, transportation, and more, plus Spanish and French survival phrases.

To travel smartly, read this little book in its entirety before you go. It's my hope that this guide will make your trip more meaningful and rewarding. Traveling like a temporary local, you'll get the absolute most out of every mile, minute, and dollar.

Buen viaje and *bon voyage!*

Rick Steves

BASQUE COUNTRY

Euskal Herria

Straddling two nations on the Atlantic Coast—stretching about 100 miles from Bilbao, Spain, north to Bayonne, France—lies the ancient, free-spirited land of the Basques. The Basque Country is famous for its sunny beaches and scintillating modern architecture...and for its feisty, industrious natives. It's also simply beautiful: Bright white chalet-style homes with deep-red and green shutters scatter across lush, rolling hills; the Pyrenees Mountains soar high above the Atlantic; and surfers and sardines share the waves.

Insulated from mainstream Europe for much of their history, the plucky Basques have wanted to be left alone for more than 7,000 years. An easily crossed border separates the French *Pays Basque* from the Spanish *País Vasco,* allowing you to sample both sides from a single base (in Spain, I prefer fun-loving San Sebastián; in France, I hang my beret in cozy St-Jean-de-Luz).

Much unites the Spanish and French Basque regions: They share a cuisine, Union Jack-style flag (green, red, and white), and common language (Euskara), spoken by about a half-million people. (Virtually everyone also speaks Spanish and/or French.) And both have been integrated by their respective nations, sometimes forcibly. The French Revolution quelled French Basque ideas of independence; 130 years later, Spain's fascist dictator, Generalísimo Francisco Franco, attempted to tame his own separatist-minded Basques.

But over the past few generations, things have started looking up. The long-suppressed Euskara language is enjoying a resurgence. And, as the European Union celebrates ethnic regions rather than nations, the Spanish and French Basques are feeling

Basque Country at a Glance

▲▲**San Sebastián (Spain)** Relaxing upscale city with beachfront promenade wrapped around chic shopping neighborhood and tasty tapas bars.

▲▲**Bilbao (Spain)** Revitalized regional capital with architectural gem—Guggenheim Bilbao—and atmospheric Old Town.

▲▲**St-Jean-de-Luz (France)** Sleepy seaside retreat in the French *Pays Basque* that serves as home base for countryside exploration.

▲**Guernica (Spain)** Village at the heart of Basque culture that was devastated by bombs during the Spanish Civil War—later immortalized by Picasso masterpiece.

▲**Bayonne (France)** Urban French scene with a Basque twist, home to impressive cultural museum, scenic ramparts, and lots of ham.

Biarritz (France) Beach resort known for its mix of international glitz and surfer dudes.

more united. This heavily industrialized region is enjoying a striking 21st-century renaissance. In Spain, the dazzling architecture of the Guggenheim Bilbao modern-art museum and the glittering resort of San Sebastián are drawing enthusiastic crowds. And in France, long-ignored cities such as Bayonne and the surfing mecca of Biarritz are being revitalized. At the same time, traditional small towns—like Spain's Lekeitio and Hondarribia, and France's St-Jean-de-Luz and nearby mountain villages—are also thriving, making the entire region colorful, fun, welcoming...and unmistakably Basque.

PLANNING YOUR TIME

One day is enough for a quick sample of the Basque Country, but two or three days lets you breathe deep and hold it in. Where you go depends on your interests: Spain or France? Cities (such as Bilbao and Bayonne) or resorts (such as San Sebastián and St-Jean-de-Luz)?

If you want to slow down and focus on Spain, spend one day relaxing in San Sebastián and the second side-tripping to Bilbao (and Guernica, if you have a car).

Better yet, take this easy opportunity to dip into France. Sleep in one country, then side-trip into the other, devoting one day

to Spain (San Sebastián and maybe Bilbao), and a second day to France (St-Jean-de-Luz and Bayonne).

Wherever you go, your Basque sightseeing should be a fun blend of urban, rural, cultural, and culinary activities.

GETTING AROUND THE BASQUE COUNTRY

The tourist's Basque Country—from Bilbao to Bayonne—stays close to the coastline. Fortunately, everything is connected by good roads and public transportation.

By Bus and Train: From San Sebastián, the bus is the best way to reach Bilbao (and from there, Guernica). To go between San Sebastián and France, a train—with a transfer in Hendaye—is your best bet. Once in France, the three main towns (St-Jean-de-Luz, Bayonne, and Biarritz) are connected by bus and by train. Even if you rent a car, I'd do these three towns by public transit. Specific connections are explained in each section.

Note that a few out-of-the-way areas—Spain's Bay of Biscay and France's Basque villages of the interior—are impractical by public transportation...but worth the trouble by car.

By Car: San Sebastián, Bilbao, St-Jean-de-Luz, and Bayonne are connected by a convenient expressway, called A-8 in Spain and A-63 in France (rough timings: Bilbao to San Sebastián, 1.25 hours; San Sebastián to St-Jean-de-Luz, 45 minutes; St-Jean-de-Luz to Bayonne, 30 minutes).

Language Warning: For the headers throughout this chapter, I've listed place names using the Spanish or French spelling first and the Euskara spelling second. In the text, I use the spelling that prevails locally. While most people refer to towns by their Spanish or French names, many road signs list places in Euskara. (In Spain, signs are usually posted in both Euskara and Spanish, either on the same sign or with dual signage on opposite sides of the street. In less separatist-minded France, signs are often only in French.) The Spanish or French version is sometimes scratched out by locals, so you might have to navigate by Euskara names.

Also note that in terms of linguistic priority (e.g., museum information), Euskara comes first, Spanish and French tie for second, and English a distant fourth...and it often doesn't make the cut.

Who Are the Basques?

To call the Basques "mysterious" is an understatement. Before most European nations had ever set sail, Basque whalers competed with the Vikings for control of the sea. During the Industrial Revolution and lean Franco years, Basque steel kept the Spanish economy alive. In the last few decades, the separatist group ETA has given the Basque people an unwarranted reputation for violence. And through it all, the Basques have spoken a unique language that to outsiders sounds like gibberish or a secret code.

So just who are the Basques? Even for Basques, that's a difficult question. According to traditional stereotypes, Basques are thought of as having long noses, heavy eyebrows, floppy ears, stout bodies, and a penchant for wearing berets. But widespread Spanish and French immigration has made it difficult to know who actually has Basque ethnic roots. (In fact, some of the Basques' greatest patriots have had no Basque blood.) And so today, anyone who speaks the Basque language, Euskara, is considered a "Basque."

Euskara, related to no other surviving tongue, has been used since Neolithic times—making it, very likely, the oldest European language that's still spoken. With its seemingly impossible-to-pronounce words filled with k's, tx's, and z's (restrooms are *komunak*: *gizonak* for men and *emakumeak* for women), Euskara makes speaking Spanish suddenly seem easy. (Some tips: *tx* is pronounced "ch" and *tz* is pronounced "ts." Other key words: *kalea* is "street," and *ostatua* is a cheap hotel.) Kept alive as a symbol of Basque cultural identity, Euskara typically is learned proudly as a second or third language. Many locals can switch effortlessly from Euskara to Spanish or French.

The Basque economy has historically been shaped by three factors: the sea, agriculture, and iron deposits.

Basque sailors were some of the first and finest in Europe, as they built ever-better boats to venture farther and farther into the Atlantic in search of whales. By the year 1000, Basque sailors were chasing whales a thousand miles from home, in the Norwegian fjords.

Despite lack of physical evidence, many historians surmise that the Basques must have sailed to Newfoundland long before Christopher Columbus landed in the Caribbean.

When the "Spanish" era of exploration began, Basques continued to play a key role, as sailors and shipbuilders. Columbus' *Santa María* was likely Basque-built, and his crew included many Basques. History books teach that Ferdinand Magellan was the first to circumnavigate the globe, with the footnote that he was killed partway around. Who took over the helm for the rest of the journey, completing the circle? It was his Basque captain, Juan Sebastián de Elcano. And a pair of well-traveled Catholic priests, known for their far-reaching missionary trips that led to founding the Jesuit order, were also Basques: St. Ignatius of Loyola and St. Francis Xavier.

Later, the Industrial Age swept Europe, gaining a foothold in Iberia when the Basques began using their rich iron deposits to make steel. Pioneering Basque industrialists set the tempo as they dragged Spain into the modern world. Cities such as Bilbao were heavily industrialized, sparking an influx of workers from around Spain (which gradually diluted Basque blood in the Basque Country).

The independence-minded Basques are notorious for their stubbornness. In truth, as a culturally and linguistically unique

island surrounded by bigger and stronger nations, the Basques have learned to compromise. Historically Basques have remained on good terms with outsiders, so long as their traditional laws, the *Fueros*, were respected. Though outdated, the *Fueros* continue to symbolize a self-governance that the Basques hold dear. It is only when foreign law has been placed above the *Fueros*—as many of today's Basques feel Spanish law is—that the people become agitated.

In recent years, much of the news of the Basques—especially in Spain—was made by the terrorist organization ETA, whose goal has been to establish an independent Basque state. (ETA stands for the Euskara phrase "Euskadi Ta Askatasuna," or "Basque Country and Freedom.") ETA has been blamed for more than 800 deaths since 1968, but in late 2011, the group declared an end to its campaign of violence (but not its call for independence). While many people in the Basque Country would like a greater degree of autonomy from Madrid, only a tiny minority of the population supports ETA, and the vast majority rejects violence.

This is only a first glimpse into the important, quirky, and fascinating Basque people. To better understand the Basques, there's no better book than Mark Kurlansky's *The Basque History of the World*—essential pre-trip reading for historians. And various museums in this region also illuminate Basque culture and history, including the Museum of San Telmo in San Sebastián (see page 18), the Assembly House and Basque Country Museum in Guernica (page 41), and the Museum of Basque Culture in Bayonne (page 93).

CUISINE SCENE IN THE BASQUE COUNTRY

Mixing influences from the mountains, sea, Spain, and France, Basque food is reason enough to visit the region. The local cuisine—dominated by seafood, tomatoes, and red peppers—offers some spicy dishes, unusual in most of Europe. And though you'll find similar specialties throughout the Basque lands, Spain is still Spain and France is still France. Here are some dishes you're most likely to find in each area.

Spanish Basque Cuisine: Hopping from bar to bar sampling *pintxos*—the local term for tapas—is a highlight of any trip. Local brews include *sidra* (hard apple cider) and *txakolí* (chah-koh-LEE, a light, sparkling white wine—often theatrically poured from high above the glass for aeration). You'll want to sample the famous *pil-pil,* made from emulsifying the skin of *bacalao* (dried, salted cod) into a mayonnaise-like substance with chili and garlic. Another tasty dish is *kokotxas,* usually made from hake *(merluza)* fish cheeks, prepared like *pil-pil,* and cooked slowly over a low heat so the natural gelatin is released, turning it into a wonderful sauce—*¡qué bueno!* Look also for white asparagus from Navarra. Wine-wise, I prefer the reds and rosés from Navarra. Finish your dinner with *cuajada,* a yogurt-like, creamy milk dessert that's sometimes served with honey and nuts. Another specialty, found throughout Spain, is *membrillo,* a sweet and *muy* dense quince jelly. Try it with cheese for a light dessert, or look for it at breakfast.

French Basque Cuisine: The red peppers (called *piments d'Espelette*) hanging from homes in small villages give foods a distinctive flavor and often end up in *piperade,* a dish that combines peppers, tomatoes, garlic, ham, and eggs. Peppers are also dried and used as condiments. Look for them with the terrific Basque dish *axoa* (a veal or lamb stew on mashed potatoes). Look also for anything "Basque-style" *(basquaise)*—cooked with tomato, eggplant, red pepper, and garlic. Don't leave without trying *ttoro* (tchoo-roh), a seafood stew that is the Basque Country's answer to bouillabaisse and cioppino. *Marmitako* is a hearty tuna stew. Local cheeses come from Pyrenean sheep's milk *(pur brebis),* and the local ham *(jambon de Bayonne)* is famous throughout France. After dinner try a shot of *izarra* (herbal-flavored brandy). To satisfy your sweet tooth, look for *gâteau basque,* a local tart filled with pastry cream or cherries from Bayonne. Hard apple cider is a tasty and local beverage. The regional wine Irouléguy comes in red, white, and rosé, and is the only wine produced in the French part of Basque Country (locals like to say that it's made from the smallest vineyard in France but the biggest in the Northern Basque Country).

Spanish Basque Country (El País Vasco)

Four of the seven Basque territories lie within Spain. Many consider Spanish Basque culture to be feistier and more colorful than the relatively assimilated French Basques—you'll hear more Euskara spoken here than in France.

For nearly 40 years, beginning in 1939, the figure of Generalísimo Franco loomed large over the Spanish Basques. Franco depended upon Basque industry to keep the floundering Spanish economy afloat. But even as he exploited the Basques economically, he so effectively blunted Basque culture that the language was primarily Spanish by default. Franco kicked off his regime by offering up the historic Basque town of Guernica as target practice to Hitler's air force. The notorious result—the wholesale slaughter of innocent civilians—was immortalized by Pablo Picasso's mural *Guernica*.

But Franco is long gone, and today's Basques are looking to the future. The iron deposits have been depleted, prompting the Basques to re-imagine their rusting cities for the 21st century. True to form, they're rising to the challenge. Perhaps the best example is Bilbao, whose iconic Guggenheim Museum—built on the former site of an industrial wasteland—is the centerpiece of a bold new skyline.

San Sebastián is the heart of the tourist's *País Vasco*, with its sparkling, picturesque beach framed by looming green mountains and a charming Old Town with gourmet *pintxos* (tapas) spilling out of every bar. On-the-rise Bilbao is worth a look for its landmark Guggenheim and its atmospheric Old Town. For small-town fun, drop by the fishing village of Lekeitio (near Bilbao). And for history, Guernica has some intriguing museums.

This chapter focuses on Basque destinations on or near the ocean.

San Sebastián / Donostia

Shimmering above the breathtaking Concha Bay, elegant and prosperous San Sebastián (Donostia in Euskara, which locals lovingly shorten to Donosti) has a favored location with golden beaches, capped by twin peaks at either end, and with a cute little island in the center. A delightful beachfront promenade runs the length of the bay, with a charismatic Old Town at one end and a smart shopping district in the center. It has 186,000 residents and almost that many tourists in high season (July-Sept). With a romantic setting, a soaring statue of Christ gazing over the city, and a late-night lively Old Town, San Sebastián has a mini Rio de Janeiro aura. Though the actual "sightseeing" isn't much, the scenic city itself provides a pleasant introduction to Spain's Basque Country. As a culinary capital

of Spain—with many local restaurants getting international attention—competition is tight to dish up some of the top tapas anywhere. And because it will be a European Capital of Culture in 2016, the city has been spiffing up its public spaces and museums.

In 1845, Queen Isabel II's doctor recommended she treat her skin problems by bathing here in the sea. (For modesty's sake, she would go inside a giant cabana that could be wheeled into the surf—allowing her to swim far from prying eyes, never having to set foot on the beach.) Her visit mobilized Spain's aristocracy, and soon the city was on the map as a seaside resort. By the turn of the 20th century, San Sebastián was the toast of the belle époque, and a leading resort for Europe's beautiful people. Before World War I, Queen María Cristina summered here and held court in her Miramar Palace overlooking the crescent beach (the turreted, red-brick building partway around the bay). Hotels, casinos, and theaters flourished. Even Franco enjoyed 35 summers in a place he was sure to call San Sebastián, not Donostia.

PLANNING YOUR TIME

San Sebastián's sights can be exhausted in a few hours, but it's a great place to be on vacation for a full, lazy day (or longer). Stroll the two-mile-long promenade with the locals and scout the place you'll grab to work on a tan. The promenade leads to a funicular that lifts you to the Monte Igueldo viewpoint. After exploring the Old Town and port, walk up to the hill of Monte Urgull. If you have more time, enjoy the delightful aquarium or the free history museum inside Monte Urgull's old castle. Or check out the Museum of San Telmo, the largest of its kind on Basque culture, which tracks the evolution of this unique society with state-of-the-art displays. A key ingredient of any visit to San Sebastián is enjoying tapas (*pintxos*) in the Old Town bars.

Orientation to San Sebastián

The San Sebastián that we're interested in surrounds Concha Bay (Bahía de la Concha). It can be divided into three areas: Playa de la

Concha (best beaches), the shopping district (called Centro), and the skinny streets of the grid-planned Old Town (called Parte Vieja, to the north of the shopping district). Centro, just east of Playa de la Concha, has beautiful turn-of-the-20th-century architecture, but no real sights. A busy drag called Alameda del Boulevard (or just "Boulevard") stands where the city wall once ran, and separates the Centro from the Old Town.

It's all bookended by mini-mountains: Monte Urgull to the north and east, and Monte Igueldo to the south and west. The river (Río Urumea) divides central San Sebastián from the district called Gros, with a lively night scene and surfing beach.

TOURIST INFORMATION

San Sebastián's TI, conveniently located right on the Boulevard, has information on city and regional sights, bike rentals (see "Helpful Hints," later), and bus and train schedules. Pick up the free map and various pamphlets with English descriptions of three self-guided walking tours—the Old Town/Monte Urgull walk is best. The TI also offers guided walking tours (July-Sept Mon-Sat 9:00-20:00, Sun 10:00-19:00; Oct-June Mon-Thu 9:00-13:30 & 15:30-19:00, Fri-Sat 10:00-19:00, Sun 10:00-14:00; Boulevard 8, tel. 943-481-166, www.sansebastianturismo.com).

ARRIVAL IN SAN SEBASTIÁN

By Train: The town has two train stations (neither has luggage storage, but you can leave bags at Navi.net Internet café downtown—see "Helpful Hints," later).

If you're coming on a regional train from Hendaye/Hendaia on the French border, get off at the **Amara EuskoTren Station** (five stops before the end of the line, which is called Lasarte-Oria). It's a level 15-minute walk to the center: Exit the station and walk across the long plaza, then veer right and walk eight blocks down Calle Easo (toward the statue of Christ hovering on the hill) to the beach. The Old Town will be ahead on your right, with Playa de la Concha to your left. To speed things up, catch bus #21, #26, or #28 along Calle Easo and take it to the Boulevard stop, near the TI at the bottom of the Old Town.

If you're arriving by train from elsewhere in Spain (or from France after transferring in Irún), you'll get off at the main **RENFE station.** It's just across the river from the Centro shopping district. There are no convenient buses from the station—to get to the Old Town and most recommended hotels, catch a taxi (they wait out front, €6.20 to downtown). Or just walk (about 10-15 minutes)—beyond the tree-lined plaza, cross the fancy dragon-decorated María Cristina Bridge, turn right onto the busy avenue called Paseo de los Fueros, and follow the Urumea River until the last bridge. The modern, blocky Kursaal Conference Center across the river serves as an easy landmark.

By Bus: A few buses—such as those from Hondarribia and the airport—can let you off at pretty Plaza de Gipuzkoa (first stop after crossing the river, in Centro shopping area, one block from the Boulevard, TI, and Old Town). But most buses—including those from Bilbao—take you instead to San Sebastián's makeshift "bus station" (dubbed Amara) at a big roundabout called Plaza Pío XII. It's basically a parking lot with a few bus shelters and a TI kiosk (open July-Aug only). At the end of the lot nearest the big roundabout, you'll see directional signs pointing you toward the town center (about a 30-minute walk). To save time and energy, catch local bus #21, #26, or #28 from the bus stop at the start of Avenida de Sancho el Sabio and get off at the Boulevard stop, near the TI at the start of the Old Town (€1.65, pay driver).

By Plane: San Sebastián Airport (airport code: EAS) is beautifully situated along the harbor in the nearby town of Hondarribia, 12 miles east of the city, just across the bay from France (tel. 902-404-704, www.aena.es). An easy regional bus (#E21) connects the airport to San Sebastián's Plaza de Gipuzkoa, just a block south of the Boulevard and TI (€2.30, pay driver, about hourly Mon-Sat 6:00-20:15, Sun 9:40-20:55, 35 minutes, www.ekialdebus.net). Buses #E25 and #E27 also connect the airport to San Sebastián, but #E21 is much faster. A taxi into town costs about €35.

If you arrive at **Bilbao (Loiu) Airport** (airport code: BIO), go out front and take the Pesa bus directly to San Sebastián (€16.85, pay driver, runs hourly 7:45-23:45, 1.25 hours, drops off at Amara bus station; return buses run hourly 5:00-21:00, buy ticket *to* the airport at Pesa office in San Sebastián at Avenida de Sancho el Sabio 33; www.pesa.net).

By Car: Take the Amara freeway exit, follow *centro ciudad* signs into the city center, and park in a pay lot (many are well-signed—the Kursaal underground lot is the most central). If you're picking up or returning a rental car, you'll find Europcar at the RENFE train station (tel. 943-322-304). Less centrally located are Hertz (Centro Comercial Garbera, Travesía de Garbera 1, bus #16 connects with downtown, tel. 943-392-223) and Avis (a taxi ride away at Hotel Barceló Costa Vasca, Pío Baroja 15, tel. 943-461-556).

HELPFUL HINTS

Internet Access: A half-dozen Internet cafés located throughout the Old Town offer fast access for about €2/hour. Try **Navi.net** at Calle Narrica 12 (Mon-Fri 9:00-22:00, Sat-Sun 10:00-22:00; shorter hours and closed Sun off-season). Government-subsidized Wi-Fi access is widely available just about everywhere (including at most hotels).

Bookstore: Elkar, an advocate of Basque culture and literature, has two branches on the same street in the Old Town. Both have a collection of Basque literature, and one has a wide selection of guidebooks, maps, and books in English (Mon-Sat 10:00-14:00 & 16:30-20:30, Sun 11:00-14:00 & 16:30-20:30, Calle Fermín Calbetón 21 and 30, tel. 943-420-080).

Baggage Storage: There's no baggage storage at the train or bus stations. **Navi.net** Internet café, listed above, has space for about 80 bags (first-come, first-served; €0.50/hour, €5/6-24 hours).

Laundry: In the Old Town, try **5 à Sec** on the underground level of the smaller building of **Bretxa Market** (drop-off service-€13/load, same-day service if dropped off by 14:00, Mon-Sat 9:30-21:30, closed Sun; tel. 943-432-044). **Wash & Dry** is in the Gros neighborhood, across the river (self-service-€14/load, daily 8:00-22:00; drop-off service-€22/load, Mon-Fri 9:30-13:00 & 16:00-20:00; Iparragirre 6, tel. 943-293-150).

Bike Rental: The city has some great bike lanes and is a good place to enjoy on two wheels. (But pedestrians need to be careful—never stand in bike lanes at intersections.) Like many cities in Europe, San Sebastián has an automated bike-sharing program, but the program is in flux and is geared toward locals. Instead, try **Sanse Bikes** near the City Hall (€5/hour, €12/half-day; Boulevard 25, tel. 943-945-229). Another option is **Bici Rent Donosti** (also rents scooters in summer, Avenida de Zurriola 22, three blocks across river from TI, mobile 639-016-013.

Marijuana: While Spain is famously liberal about marijuana laws, the Basque Country is even more so. Walking around San Sebastián, you'll see "grow shops" sporting the famous green leaf (shopkeepers are helpful if you have questions). The sale of marijuana is still illegal, but the consumption of marijuana is decriminalized and people are allowed to grow enough for their personal use at home. With the town's mesmerizing aquarium and delightfully lit bars filled with enticing munchies, it just makes sense here.

GETTING AROUND SAN SEBASTIÁN

By Bus: Along the Boulevard at the bottom edge of the Old Town, you'll find a line of public buses ready to take you anywhere in town; give any driver your destination, and he or she will tell you the number of the bus to catch (€1.65, pay driver).

Some handy bus routes: #21, #26, and #28 connect the Amara bus station and Amara EuskoTren Station to the TI (get off at the Boulevard stop); #5, #16, and #25 begin at the Boulevard/TI stop, go along Playa de la Concha and through residential areas; #16 eventually arrives at the base of the Monte Igueldo funicular (for bus info, see www.dbus.es).

By Taxi: Taxis start at €6.20, which covers most rides in the center. You can't hail a taxi on the street—you must call one (tel. 943-404-040 or 943-464-646) or find a taxi stand (most convenient along the Boulevard).

By Metro: A new subway system is currently under construction in San Sebastián. Officials are also upgrading San Sebastián's EuskoTren line. It'll eventually be renamed, but for now, locals continue to call it by its nickname—Topo ("Mole")—because it goes underground part of the time.

Tours in San Sebastián

Walking Tours

The TI runs English-language walking tours. Options include Essential San Sebastián (€10, 2 hours), *Pintxos* of San Sebastián (€18, 2 hours, includes three *pintxos* and three drinks), Romantic San Sebastián (through the elegant Centro district, €10, 2 hours), and—during the September film festival—San Sebastián: A Film City (€14, 2 hours, includes one *pintxo* and one drink). Schedules vary—ask at the TI, call 943-217-717, or check www.sansebastian reservas.com for info and reservations.

Local Guides

Itsaso Petrikorena is good (mobile 647-973-231, betitsaso@yahoo.es). Gabriella Ranelli, an American who's lived in San Sebastián for over 20 years, specializes in culinary tours. She can take you on a sightseeing spin around the Old Town, along with a walk through the market and best *pintxo* bars (€185/half-day, €395/day, higher depending on destinations, transportation included for up to four people, mobile 609-467-381, www.tenedortours.com, info@tenedortours.com). Gabriella also organizes cooking classes—where you shop at the market, then join a local chef to cook up some tasty *pintxos* of your own (€135/person for a small group)—as well as wine-tastings (start at €55/person).

Gastronomic Tours

San Sebastián Food offers travelers the opportunity to enter one of San Sebastián's exclusive "private eating clubs" and even participate in preparing a gourmet meal. Prices start around €120 per person (4-person minimum), including ingredients and wine. They also organize €90 *pintxo* tours that have you hopping from bar to bar (includes food and wine) and €90 Iberian ham-cutting courses with sherry tasting (3-person minimum; Paseo Republica Argentina 4, tel. 943-421-143, www.sansebastianfood.com, info@sansebastianfood.com).

Tours on Wheels

Two tour options on wheels (following a similar route around the bay) are available, but most travelers won't find them necessary in this walkable city: the **"txu-txu"** tourist train (€5, daily July-mid-Sept 10:30-21:00, mid-Sept-June 11:00-18:30, closed Jan-Feb and Mon off-season, 40-minute round-trip, tel. 943-422-973), and the **Donosti Tours** hop-on, hop-off bus tour along the bay and around the city (€12, one-hour loop, ticket valid 24 hours, leaves from Victoria Eugenia theater on the Boulevard, tel. 943-441-828, www.busturistikoa.com, Raquel).

Basque Excursions

Based in San Sebastián, **Agustin Ciriza** leads walking tours of his hometown and guided tours through the Spanish and French Basque Country, with destinations including Bilbao, Hondarribia, Biarritz, the Biscay Coast, Bayonne, and Pamplona (even during the running of the bulls). He also offers guided kayaking expeditions, Camino pilgrimages, mountain treks, surf lessons, surfing trips, and Rioja region wine tours, as well as wine tastings, food tours, and cooking classes in town. Prices start at €25 for city tours (4-person minimum) and €75 for a half-day excursion (2-person minimum; mobile 686-117-395, www.gorilla-trip.com, agus@gorilla-trip.com).

Sights in San Sebastián

▲▲OLD TOWN (PARTE VIEJA)

Huddled in the shadow of its once-protective Monte Urgull, the Old Town is where San Sebastián was born about 1,000 years ago. Because the town burned down in 1813 (as Spain, Portugal, and England fought the French to get Napoleon's brother off the Spanish throne), the architecture you see is generally Neoclassical and uniform. Still, the grid plan of streets hides heavy Baroque and Gothic churches, surprise plazas, and fun little shops, including venerable pastry stores, rugged produce markets, Basque-

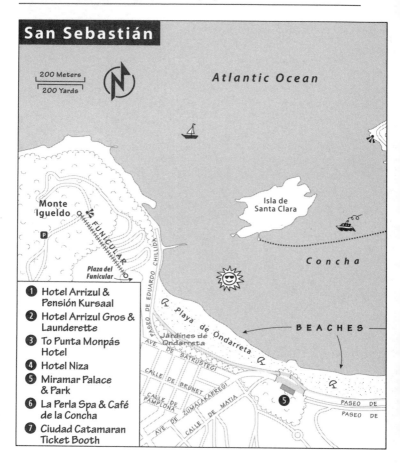

San Sebastián

200 Meters
200 Yards

N

Atlantic Ocean

Monte Igueldo

FUNICULAR

P

Plaza del Funicular

PASEO DE EDUARDO CHILLIDA

Isla de Santa Clara

Concha

☀

Playa de Ondarreta

Jardines de Ondarreta

AVE DE SATRUSTEGI

CALLE DE BRUNET

CALLE DE PAMPLONA

AVE DE ZUMALAKARREGI

CALLE DE MATIA

BEACHES

PASEO DE

PASEO DE

❶ Hotel Arrizul & Pensión Kursaal
❷ Hotel Arrizul Gros & Launderette
❸ To Punta Monpás Hotel
❹ Hotel Niza
❺ Miramar Palace & Park
❻ La Perla Spa & Café de la Concha
❼ Ciudad Catamaran Ticket Booth

independence souvenir shops, and seafood-to-go delis. The highlight of the Old Town is its array of incredibly lively tapas bars—though here these snacks are called *pintxos* (PEEN-chohs). To see the fishing industry in action, wander out to the port.

Although the struggle for Basque independence is currently in a relatively calm stage, with most people opposing violent ETA tactics, there are still underlying tensions between Spain and the Basque people. In the middle of the Old Town, **Calle Juan de Bilbao** is the political-action street. Here you'll find people more sympathetic to the struggle (whereas for others, it's a street to avoid). Speaking Euskara is encouraged.

Throughout the Old Town, flagpoles mark **"private eating clubs"** (you might occasionally see a club's name displayed, but most are otherwise unmarked). The clubs used to be exclusively male; women are now allowed as invited guests...but never in the kitchen, which remains the men's domain. Basque society is matri-

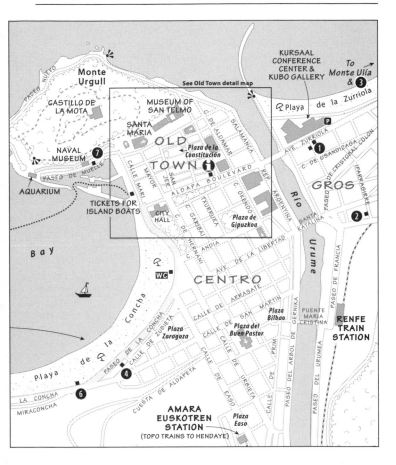

lineal and very female-oriented. A husband brings home his pay-check and hands it directly to his wife, who controls the house's purse strings (and everything else). Basque men felt they needed a place where they could congregate and play "king of the castle," so they formed these clubs where members could reserve a table and cook for their friends.

▲Plaza de la Constitución

The Old Town's main square is where bullfights used to be held. Notice the seat numbering on the balconies: Even if you owned an apartment here, the city retained rights to the balconies, which

it could sell as box seats. (Residents could peek over the paying customers' shoulders.) Above the clock, notice the seal of San Sebastián: a merchant ship with sails billowing in the wind. The city was granted trading rights by the crown—a reminder of the Basque Country's importance in Spanish seafaring. Inviting café tables spill into the square from all corners.

▲▲Museum of San Telmo (San Telmo Museoa)

A recent addition to this fascinating museum innovatively wrapped a modern facade around a 16th-century Dominican convent and its peaceful cloister. It's now the largest museum of Basque culture in the country and is well worth a visit. Exhibits of archaeological and ethnographic artifacts demonstrate the traditional folkways of Basque life and vividly tell the history of the region. Its art collection features a few gems (El Greco, Rubens, Tintoretto), while 19th- and 20th-century paintings by Basque artists offer an interesting peek into the spirit, faces, and natural beauty of these fiercely independent people. While individual displays lack explanations in English, portable placards are available, providing a sufficient overview.

Cost and Hours: €6, free on Tue, open Tue-Sun 10:00-20:00, closed Mon, Plaza Zuloaga 1, tel. 943-481-580, www.santelmo museoa.com.

Visiting the Museum: Section 1, within the church of the original convent, houses 11 exceptional varnish-on-metal paintings by Spanish artist José María Sert; the light reflecting off this artwork bathes the church in a hauntingly warm glow. Commissioned in 1929, when the convent was originally converted into a museum, these "Sert Canvases" are passionate depictions of epic Basque moments and traditions.

Breeze through Section 2, which features steles or funerary markers, and tuck into Section 3, where traditional Basque tools and time-honored apparel are smartly displayed. A fine ship model is part of a high-tech exhibit illustrating the far reaches of seafaring Basque explorers.

Continue upstairs to Section 4, where you'll have an eye-level peek at the Sert Canvases. You'll also learn how the Basque people transitioned from a rural lifestyle to urban modernity in the 19th and 20th centuries.

Paintings from the 15th to 19th centuries are displayed in Section 5 on the top-most floor, giving you a chronological glimpse of respectable works from several well-known (and many lesser-known) Spanish artists.

▲Bretxa Public Market (Mercado de la Bretxa)

Wandering through the public market is a fun way to get in touch with San Sebastián and Basque culture. Although the sandstone market building facing the Boulevard and the large, former Pescadería building have both been converted into a modern shopping complex, the farmers' produce market thrives here (lined up outside along the left side of the mall), as does the fish and meat market (underground).

Hours: Mon-Fri 8:00-14:00 & 17:00-20:00, Sat 8:00-14:00, closed Sun, Bretxa Plaza.

Visiting the Market: To get to the modern fish and meat market, walk past the produce vendors (look under the eaves of the building to see what the farmers are selling), and find a big glass cube in the square, where an escalator takes you down into the market.

At the bottom of the escalator, notice the **fish stall** on the left (marked *J. Ma. Mujika*). In the case, you'll see different cuts of *bacalao* (cod). Entire books have been written about the importance of cod to the evolution of seafaring in Europe. The fish could be preserved in salt to feed sailors on ever-longer trips into the North Atlantic, allowing them to venture beyond the continental shelf (into deeper waters where they couldn't catch fresh fish). Cod was also popular among Catholic landlubbers on Fridays. Today cod remains a Basque staple. People still buy the salted version, which must be soaked for 48 hours (and the water changed three times) to become edible. If you're in a rush, you can buy de-salted cod...but at a cost in flavor. Stroll behind this stall to explore the fresh fish market--often with the catch of the day set up in cute little scenes. Few fish stands are open on Monday, because boats don't go out on Sunday; even fishermen need a day off. There's a free **WC** in the market—just ask *"¿Dónde está el servicio, por favor?"*

When you're done exploring, take the escalator up, turn left, and cross the street to the **Aitor Lasa** cheese shop (Mon-Fri 8:30-14:00 & 17:15-20:00, Sat 8:30-14:30, closed Sun, Aldamar 12, tel. 943-430-354). Pass the fragrant piles of mushrooms at the entrance and head back to the display case, showing off the Basque specialty of *idiazábal*—raw sheep's milk cheese. Notice the wide variety, which depends on the specific region it came from, whether it's smoked or cured, and for how long it's been cured *(curación)*. If you're planning a picnic, this is a very local (and expensive) ingredient. To try the cheese that won first prize a few years back in the Ordizia International Cheese Competition, ask for *"El queso con el premio de Ordizia, por favor."* The owners are evangelical about the magic of combining the local cheese with walnuts and *casero* (homemade) apple jam.

THE PORT

At the west end of the Old Town, protected by Monte Urgull, is the port. Take the passage through the wall at the appropriately

named Calle Puerto, and jog
right along the level, portside
promenade, Paseo del Muelle.
You'll pass fishing boats
unloading the catch of the
day (with hungry locals looking on), salty sailors' pubs, and
fishermen mending nets. Also
along this strip are the skip-

pable Naval Museum and the entertaining aquarium. Trails to the
top of Monte Urgull are just above this scene, near Santa María
Church (or climb the stairs next to the aquarium).

Cruises

Small boats cruise from the Old Town's port to the island in the
bay (Isla Santa Clara), where you can hike the trails and have lunch
at the lone café, or pack a picnic before setting sail. **Motoras de la
Isla** offers two different options: the direct red *(roja)* route to the
island (€3.80 round-trip, small ferry departs June-Sept only, every
half-hour 10:00-20:00) and the blue *(azul)* route, which cruises the
bay for 25 minutes in a glass-bottom boat before dropping passengers off (€6 round-trip, hourly 11:00-19:30; tel. 943-000-045,
www.motorasdelaisla.com). The *Ciudad San Sebastián* catamaran
gives 40-minute tours of the bay from Monte Igueldo to Zurriola
Beach (€9, in summer departs hourly 12:00-14:00 & 16:00-20:00,
fewer in spring and fall, none in winter; tel. 943-287-932, www.
ciudadsansebastian.com).

Naval Museum (Museo Naval)

This museum's two floors of exhibits describe the seafaring city's
history, revealing the intimate link between the Basque culture
and the sea.

Cost and Hours: €1.20, free on Thu, borrow English descrip-
tion at entry, Tue-Sat 10:00-14:00 & 16:00-19:00, Sun 11:00-14:00,
closed Mon, Paseo del Muelle 24, tel. 943-430-051.

▲▲Aquarium

San Sebastián's aquarium is surprisingly good. Exhibits are thoughtfully described in English and include a history of the sea, a collection of naval vessels, and models showing various drift-netting
techniques. But the real action is on the ground floor, where you'll
see a petting tank filled with nervous fish; a huge whale skeleton; a
trippy, illuminated, slowly tumbling tank of jellyfish; and a mesmerizing 45-foot-long tunnel that lets you look up into a wet world of
floppy rays, menacing sharks, and local fish. The local section ends
with a tank of shark fetuses safely incubating away from hungry
predators. Local kids see the tropical wing and holler, "Nemo!"

Cost and Hours: €13, €7 for kids under 13; July-Aug daily 10:00-21:00; Easter-June and Sept Mon-Fri 10:00-20:00, Sat-Sun 10:00-21:00; Oct-Easter Mon-Fri 10:00-19:00, Sat-Sun 10:00-20:00; last entry one hour before closing, stuffy-yet-helpful audioguide-€2, at the end of Paseo del Muelle, tel. 943-440-099, www.aquariumss.com.

▲Monte Urgull

The once-mighty castle (Castillo de la Mota) atop the hill deterred most attackers, allowing the city to prosper in the Middle Ages.

The **Casa de la Historia** museum within the castle covers San Sebastián history; it has mildly interesting displays on the ground floor and access to the statue of Christ's view over the city. There are also 13 delightful videos available in English—created for the 200th anniversary of the city's devastating fire of 1813, each eight-minute film features San Sebastián youth sharing their city's important historical moments (free to enter museum, €1 English pamphlet, open Wed-Sun 10:00-17:30, closed in winter and Mon-Tue year-round, tel. 943-428-417).

Maps scattered throughout the **park** provide good and basic information in English about the fortress. Seek out the crumbling memorial to British soldiers who gave their lives to defend the city from Napoleon. The best views from the hill are not from the statue of Christ, but from the **Battery of Santiago** ramparts (to Christ's far right), just above the port's aquarium. Picnickers can enjoy their lunch along the walls and on benches peppering the grassy battery park, or walk to the western-most point of the battery to the free-spirited **Café El Polvorín** for salads, sandwiches, good sangria, and picturesque vistas.

A walkway allows you to stroll the mountain's entire perimeter near sea level. This route is continuous from Hotel Parma to the aquarium, and offers an enjoyable after-dinner wander. You can also walk a bit higher up over the port (along the white railing)—called the *paseo de las curas,* or "priest's path," where the clergy could stroll unburdened by the rabble in the streets below. These paths are technically open only from sunrise to sunset (daily May-Sept 8:00-21:00, Oct-April 8:00-19:00), but you can often access them even later.

THE BEACH AND BEYOND
▲▲La Concha Beach and Promenade

The shell-shaped Playa de la Concha, the pride of San Sebastián, has one of Europe's loveliest stretches of sand. Lined with a two-mile-long promenade, it allows even backpackers to feel aristocratic. Although it's pretty empty off-season, sunbathers pack its shores in summer. But year-round it's surprisingly devoid of eateries and money-grubbing businesses. There are free showers, and *cabinas* provide lockers, showers, and shade for a fee. For a century, the lovingly painted wrought-iron balustrade that stretches the length of the promenade has been a symbol of the city; it shows up on every-

thing from jewelry to headboards. It's shaded by tamarisk trees, with branches carefully pruned into knotty bulbs each winter that burst into leafy shade-giving canopies in the summer—another symbol of the city. **Café de la Concha** serves reasonably priced, mediocre food, but you can't beat the location of its terrace overlooking the beach (€15 weekday lunch special, tel. 943-473-600).

The **Miramar Palace and Park** divides the crescent beach in the middle at Pico de Loro (Parrot's Beak). This is where Queen María Cristina held court when she summered here in the early 1900s. Today the palace is home to summer classes for the Basque Studies University, as well as a music school. The gardens are open to the public.

La Perla Spa

The spa overlooking the beach attracts a less royal crowd today and appeals mostly to visitors interested in sampling "the curative properties of the sea." You can enjoy its Talasso Fitness Circuit, featuring a hydrotherapy pool, a relaxation pool, a panoramic Jacuzzi, cold-water pools, a seawater steam sauna, a dry sauna, and a relaxation area.

Cost and Hours: €27 for 2-hour fitness circuit, €32 for 3-hour circuit, daily 8:00-22:00, €3 caps and €1 rental towels, bring a swimsuit or buy one for €33, on the beach at the center of the crescent, Paseo de la Concha, tel. 943-458-856, www.la-perla.net.

Monte Igueldo

For commanding city views (if you ignore the tacky amusements on top), ride the funicular up Monte Igueldo, a mirror image of Monte

Urgull. The views over San Sebastián, along the coast, and into the distant green mountains are sensational day or night. The entrance to the funicular is on the road behind the tennis club on the far western end of Playa de Ondarreta, which extends from Playa de la Concha to the west.

Cost and Hours: Funicular—€3.10 round-trip; changeable

hours but roughly April-Sept Mon-Tue and Thu-Sun 10:00-22:00, closed Wed; Oct-March Mon-Tue and Thu-Fri 11:00-18:00, Sat-Sun 11:00-20:00, closed Wed. If you drive to the top, you'll pay €2.20 to enter. Bus #16 takes you from the Old Town to the base of the funicular in about 10 minutes.

Peine del Viento

Besides the gorgeous view from the top of Monte Igueldo, another classic San Sebastián scene is at this group of three statues by native son Eduardo Chillida (1924-2002). From the base of the Monte Igueldo funicular, walk around the tennis court complex to the edge of the beach. Curly steel prongs "comb the wind" (as the sculptures' name means) among crashing waves. Chillida lived and died on Monte Igueldo, so these sculptures are now considered a memorial to one of Spain's most internationally recognized modern sculptors.

IN GROS

Gros and Zurriola Beach

The district of Gros, just east across the river from the Old Town, offers a distinct Californian vibe. Literally a dump a few years ago (gross indeed), today it has a surfing scene on Zurriola Beach (popular with students and German tourists) and a futuristic conference center (described next). Long-term plans call for a new promenade that will arc over the water and under Monte Ulía.

▲Kursaal Conference Center and Kubo Gallery

These two Lego-like boxes (just east and across the river from the Old Town, in Gros) mark the spot of what was once a grand casino, torn down by Franco to discourage gambling. Many locals wanted to rebuild it as it once was, in a similar style to the turn-of-the-20th-century buildings in the Centro, but—in an effort to keep up with the postmodern trends in Bilbao—city leaders opted instead for Rafael Moneo's striking contemporary design. The complex is supposed to resemble the angular rocks that make up the town's breakwater. The Kursaal houses a theater, conference facilities, some gift shops and travel agencies, a restaurant, and the Kubo Gallery. The gallery, located in a small cube farthest from the river, offers temporary exhibits by international artists and promotes contemporary Basque artists. Each exhibit is complemented by a 10-minute video that plays continuously in the gallery theater.

Cost and Hours: Free, Kubo Gallery open Tue-Sun 11:30-13:30 & 17:00-21:00, closed Mon, tel. 943-012-400, www.sala-kubo-aretoa.com.

Sleeping in San Sebastián

Rates in San Sebastián fluctuate with the season. When you see a range of prices in these listings, the top end is for summer (roughly July-Sept), and the low end is for the shoulder season (May-June and Oct); outside of these times, you'll pay even less. Since breakfast is often not included, I've recommended some good options elsewhere in town (see "Eating in San Sebastián," later). All of the following hotels have free Wi-Fi.

IN OR NEAR THE OLD TOWN

$$$ Hotel Parma is a business-class place with 27 fine rooms and family-run attention to detail and service. It stands stately on the edge of the Old Town, away from the bar-scene noise, and overlooks the river and a surfing beach (Sb-€71-104, windowless interior Db-€105-158, view Db-€125-172, breakfast-€11, air-con, modern lounge, Paseo de Salamanca 10, tel. 943-428-893, www. hotelparma.com, hotelparma@hotelparma.com; Iñaki, Pino, Maria Eugenia, and Eider).

$$$ Pensión AB Domini neighbors Bretxa Market and San Telmo Museum. It delightfully mixes traditional, bare-stone walls with contemporary decor. Three of its six rooms have views toward the museum—unique in the narrow-laned Old Town. With only two *pintxo* bars nearby, it's one of the quieter hotels in town, but bring earplugs for Saturdays (S-€59-65, D-€70-75, Db-€110-120, extra bed-€20; San Juan 8, second floor, tel. 943-420-431, www. abpensiones.es, reservas@abpensiones.es).

$$ Pensión Edorta ("Edward"), deep in the Old Town, elegantly mixes wood, brick, and color into nine modern, stylish rooms (D-€40-70, Db-€60-90, extra bed-€25, slightly more in Aug, elevator, Calle Puerto 15, tel. 943-423-773, www.pensione dorta.com, info@pensionedorta.com, Javier).

$$ Pensión Amaiur, in the oldest building in the Old Town, has tilting wooden stairs that lead to a flowery interior with long, narrow halls and 12 great-value rooms. Kind Virginia gives the justifiably popular *pensión* a homey warmth. Some rooms face a *frontón* (*pelota* court), while a couple have private balconies facing the street. There are common rooms on both floors to prepare meals—a great spot to hang out and share travel tips. Bring earplugs to block out noise from the tapas-going crowd, or ask for an interior room (S-€40-45, quiet interior D-€60-70, Db-€76-90, T-€80-100, Tb-€90-125, kitchen facilities, next to Santa María Church at Calle 31 de Agosto 44, tel. 943-429-654, www.pension amaiur.com, amaiur@telefonica.net).

Sleep Code

(€1 = about $1.40, Spain country code: 34, France country code: 33)

Abbreviations

S = Single, **D** = Double/Twin, **T** = Triple, **Q** = Quad, **b** = bathroom, **s** = shower only, * = French hotel rating system (0-5 stars).

Price Rankings

$$$ **Higher Priced**—Most rooms €100 or more.
$$ **Moderately Priced**—Most rooms between €60-100.
$ **Lower Priced**—Most rooms €60 or less.

Unless otherwise noted, credit cards are accepted and English is spoken, but breakfast is generally not included. The word *ostatua* (which you'll see throughout the Basque Country) means "pension." Some Spanish hotels include the 10 percent IVA tax in the room price; others tack it onto your bill. Prices change; verify current rates online or by email. For the best prices, always book directly with the hotel.

ACROSS THE RIVER, IN GROS

The pleasant Gros district—San Sebastián's "uptown"—is marked by the super-modern, blocky Kursaal conference center. The nearby Zurriola Beach is popular with surfers. Most of these hotels are less than a five-minute walk from the Old Town.

$$$ Hotel Arrizul is bright and fresh, with fashionable, minimalist decor in each of its 12 rooms (Sb-€55-105, Db-€90-145, Db suite-€110-180, extra bed-€35, breakfast-€8, air-con, elevator, nearby underground parking-€20, Peña y Goñi 1, tel. 943-322-804, www.arrizul.com, info@arrizulhotel.com). Its sister hotel, **Hotel Arrizul Gros,** is only five blocks away and has 17 rooms with similar decor (slightly lower rates, includes small breakfast) plus 15 spacious apartment rentals (apartments: 2 people-€145-199, 4 people-€185-249, 5 people-€215-279; Iparraguirre 3, same contact info as main Hotel Arrizul).

$$$ Punta Monpás Hotel is a 15-minute walk from the Old Town. Situated at the end of Zurriola Beach, its tidy and beach-chic rooms boast enviable views of the water and Monte Urgull (Sb-€100-110, Db-€120-150, Db with panoramic view-€180-200, extra bed-€20, breakfast-€8, air-con, parking-€20/day; Calle José Miguel de Barandiarán 32, tel. 943-285-585, www.puntamonpas hotel.com, reservas@puntamonpashotel.com).

$$ Pensión Kursaal has 21 basic, contemporary, and crisp rooms in a historic building (Db-€50-91, family room-€84-141, simple in-room breakfast-€4, elevator, pay guest computer, parking-€12; Peña y Goñi 2, tel. 943-292-666, www.pensionesconen canto.com, kursaal@pensionesconencanto.com).

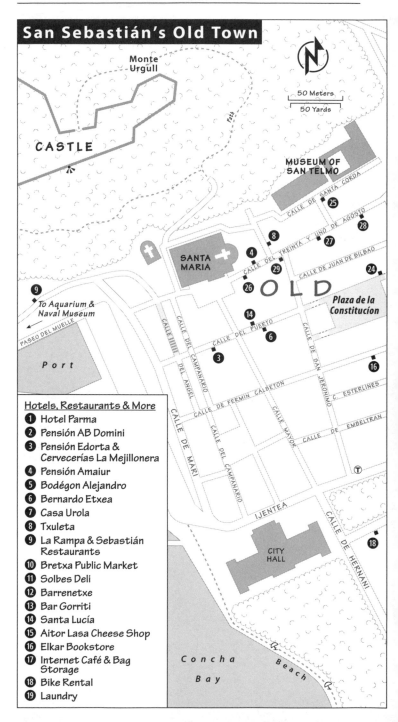

San Sebastián's Old Town

Monte Urgull

CASTLE

50 Meters
50 Yards

MUSEUM OF SAN TELMO

CALLE DE SANTA CORDA

SANTA MARIA

CALLE DEL TREINTA Y UNO DE AGOSTO

CALLE DE JUAN DE BILBAO

To Aquarium & Naval Museum

PASEO DEL MUELLE

Port

O L D

Plaza de la Constitución

CALLE DEL CAMPANARIO

CALLE DEL ANGEL

CALLE DEL PUERTO

CALLE DE SAN JERÓNIMO

C. ESTERLINES

CALLE DE FERMIN CALBETON

CALLE MAYOR

CALLE DE EMBELTRAN

CALLE DE MARI

CALLE DEL CAMPANARIO

IJENTEA

CITY HALL

CALLE DE HERNANI

Concha Bay

Beach

Hotels, Restaurants & More
1. Hotel Parma
2. Pensión AB Domini
3. Pensión Edorta & Cervecerías La Mejillonera
4. Pensión Amaiur
5. Bodégon Alejandro
6. Bernardo Etxea
7. Casa Urola
8. Txuleta
9. La Rampa & Sebastián Restaurants
10. Bretxa Public Market
11. Solbes Deli
12. Barrenetxe
13. Bar Gorriti
14. Santa Lucía
15. Aitor Lasa Cheese Shop
16. Elkar Bookstore
17. Internet Café & Bag Storage
18. Bike Rental
19. Laundry

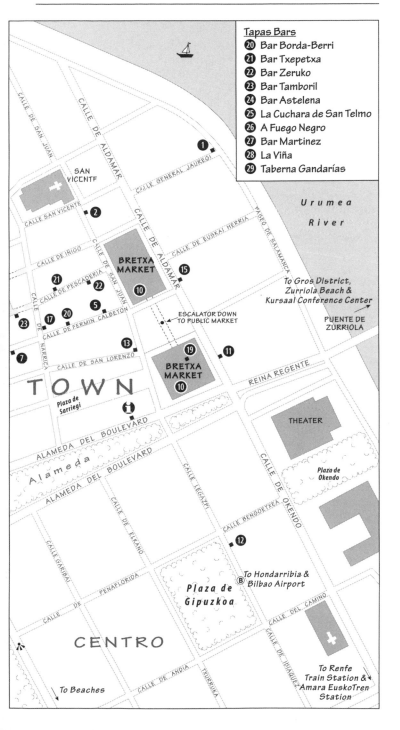

Tapas Bars
20 Bar Borda-Berri
21 Bar Txepetxa
22 Bar Zeruko
23 Bar Tamboril
24 Bar Astelena
25 La Cuchara de San Telmo
26 A Fuego Negro
27 Bar Martinez
28 La Viña
29 Taberna Gandarías

ON THE BEACH

$$$ Hotel Niza, set in the middle of Playa de la Concha, is often booked well in advance. Half of its 40 rooms (some with balconies) overlook the bay. From its chandeliered and plush lounge, a classic 1911 elevator takes you to comfortable pastel rooms with wedding-cake molding (tiny interior Sb-€55-69, Db-€132-164, view rooms cost the same—request one when you reserve...but no promises, extra bed-€24, only streetside rooms have air-con, fans on request, great buffet breakfast-€11, free guest computer, parking-€15/day—must reserve in advance, Zubieta 56, tel. 943-426-663, www.hotelniza.com, reservas@hotelniza.com.) The breakfast room has a sea view and doubles as a bar with light snacks throughout the day (Bar Narru, daily 7:30-24:00).

Eating in San Sebastián

Basque food is regarded as some of the best in Spain, and San Sebastián is the culinary capital of the Basque Country. What

the city lacks in museums and sights, it more than makes up for in food. (For tips on Basque cuisine, see page 8.) San Sebastián is proud of its many Michelin-rated fine-dining establishments, but they require a big commitment of time and money. Most casual visitors will prefer to hop from pub to pub through the Old Town, following the crowds between Basque-font signs. I've listed a couple of solid traditional restaurants, but for the best value and memories, I'd order top-end dishes with top-end wine in top-end bars. Some places close for siesta in the late afternoon and early evening.

PINTXO BAR-HOPPING IN THE OLD TOWN

San Sebastián's Old Town provides the ideal backdrop for tapas-hopping; just wander the streets and sidle up to the bar in the liveliest spot. Calle Fermín Calbetón has the best concentration of bars; the streets San Jerónimo and 31 de Agosto are also good. I've listed these top-notch

places in order as you progress deeper into the Old Town—though you have to backtrack after Bar Zeruko. Note that there are plenty of other options along the way. Before you begin, study the sidebar.

Bar Borda-Berri (loosely, "Mountain Hut") features a more low-key ambience and top-quality €3 *pintxos*. There are only a few items at the bar; check out the chalkboard menu for today's options, order, and the two chef/owners will cook it fresh. The specialty here is melt-in-your-mouth beef cheeks *(carrillera de tenera)* in a red-wine sauce, risotto with wild mushrooms, and foie gras (grilled goose liver) with apple jelly, which is even better paired with a glass of their best red wine (closed Mon, Calle Fermín Calbetón 12, tel. 943-430-342).

Bar Txepetxa is *the* place for anchovies. A plastic circle displaying a variety of *antxoas* tapas makes choosing your anchovy treat easy. These fish are fresh—not cured and salted like those most Americans hate (€2.50/*pintxo,* Tue lunch only, closed Sun-Mon, Calle Pescadería 5, tel. 943-422-227).

Bar Zeruko offers fun for molecular gastronomy fans in a bright, modern setting. The selections are seasonal, but look for *hoguera,* a piece of cod served over a smoking mini-hearth with a side of "liquid" salad. Award-winning chef Joxean Calvo continually surprises his patrons (€2-3 basic *pintxos,* €4-7.50 avant-garde *pintxos*; Tue-Sat 11:00-16:00 & 19:00-24:00, Sun 19:00-24:00, closed Mon, Calle Pescadería 10, tel. 943-423-451, www.bar zeruko.com).

Bar Tamboril is a traditional spot right on the main square favored for its seafood, mushrooms *(txampis tamboril),* and anchovy tempura along with its good prices. Their list of hot *pintxos* (grab the little English menu on the bar) makes you want to break the one-tapa-per-stop rule (Calle Pescadería 2, tel. 943-423-507).

Bar Astelena, across the square from Tamboril, serves a delicious blend of traditional and modern plates, all thoughtfully presented. Try any of the specials, particularly the *solomillo a lo pobre* (small sirloin fillet with mini-fries and a fried egg). Other standouts include *rabo de buey* (oxtail) and capellini-wrapped prawns. There's no English menu, but the staff is happy to help translate (€3-4 *pintxos,* Calle de Iñigo 1, tel. 943-425-245).

La Cuchara de San Telmo, with cooks taught by a big-name Basque chef, Alex Mondiel, is a cramped place that devotes as much space to its thriving kitchen as its bar. It has nothing precooked and set on the bar—order your mini-gourmet plates with a spirit of adventure from the constantly changing blackboard. Their foie gras with apple jelly is rightfully famous (€3.50 *pintxos,* closed Mon and Thu night, tucked away on a lonely alley called Santa Corda behind Museum of San Telmo at 31 de Agosto #28, tel. 943-435-446).

Do the *Txikiteo*: A Tapas Cheat Sheet

Txikiteo (chih-kee-TAY-oh) is the Basque word for hopping from bar to bar, enjoying small sandwiches and tiny snacks (*pintxos*, PEEN-chohs) and glasses of wine. Local competition drives small bars to lay out the most appealing array of *pintxos*. The selection is amazing, but the key to eating well here is going for the *pintxos calientes*—the hot tapas advertised on blackboards and cooked to order. Tapas are best, freshest, and accompanied by the most vibrant crowd from 12:00 to 14:00 and from 20:00 to 22:30. Watch what's being served—the locals know each bar's specialty. No matter how much you like a place, just order one dish; you want to be mobile.

Later in the evening, bars get more crowded and challenging for tourists. To get service amid the din, speak loudly and directly (little sweet voices get ignored), with no extra words. Expect to share everything. Double-dipping is encouraged. It's rude to put a dirty napkin on the table; it belongs on the floor.

Basque tapas bars distinguish themselves by laying out big platters of help-yourself goodies. This user-friendly system lets you point to—or simply take—what looks good, rather than navigating a menu. If you can't get the bartender's attention to serve you a particular *pintxo*, don't be shy—just grab it and a napkin, and munch away. You pay when you leave; just keep a mental note of the tapas you've eaten. There's a code of honor. Everyone is part of the extended Basque family. In fact, places

A Fuego Negro is cool and upscale compared with the others, with a hip, edgier vibe and a blackboard menu of *pintxos* and drinks (there's an English translation sheet). They have a knack for mixing gourmet pretentiousness with whimsy here: Try their *arroz, tomate, y un huevo* (risotto with tomato and egg); *bakailu* (cod); and *regaliz* (licorice ice cream) trio for a unique taste-bud experience (€3.60). Enjoy their serious and extensive wine selection (closed Mon, 31 de Agosto #31, tel. 650-135-373). An inviting little section in the back makes this a sit-down dining opportunity.

Cervecerías La Mejillonera is famous among students for its big, cheap beers, *patatas bravas*, and mussels ("*tigres*" is the spicy favorite). A long, skinny stainless-steel bar and lots of photos make ordering easy—this is my only recommended bar where you pay when served. Throw your mussels shells on the floor like the locals (Calle Puerto 15, tel. 943-428-465).

Bar Martinez has been around since 1942 and continues to be a go-to eatery for residents. A wide variety of options fills their long *pintxos* bar. The *piquillo* pepper with tuna, and tuna and that have you fill your plate and pay before eating are generally to be avoided.

If you want a meal instead of *pintxos*, some bars—even ones that look only like bars from the street—have attached dining rooms, usually in the back.

Here are a few terms unique to Basque bars:

pintxos: tapas (small plates)

antxoas: anchovies (not the cured, heavily salted kind you always hated)

txampis (chahm-pees): mushrooms

txangurro (chan-GOO-roh): spider crab, a delicacy, often mixed with onions, tomatoes, and wine, served hot or made into a spread to put on bread

marmitako: tuna stew

ttoro: seafood stew

cazuelas: hot meal-size servings (like raciones in Spanish)

txakoli (chah-koh-LEE): fresh white wine, poured from high to aerate it and to add sparkle. Good with seafood, and therefore fits the local cuisine well.

zurito (thoo-REE-toh): small beer

Zenbat da?: "How much?" (to ask for the bill)

bacalao with onions, are worthy standouts (daily 11:30-16:00 & 19:00-24:00, Calle 31 de Agosto 13, tel. 943-424-965).

La Viña is a reliable option for a mix of traditional and modern *pintxos*, most costing about €2. Rub elbows with locals and top off your meal with an airy and decadent slice of cheesecake that's big enough to share (daily, closed Nov and last week of June, Calle 31 de Agosto 3, tel. 943-427-495).

Taberna Gandarías is the place for savory traditional *pinxtos* in a lively, but easy-going atmosphere. The personable blue-shirted fellas tending to you will patiently help you navigate the food options. Consider a *media ración* (half-order) of the melt-in-your-mouth *Iberico* ham (€1.60-3 *pintxos*, 31 de Agosto 23, tel. 943-426-362).

RESTAURANTS IN THE OLD TOWN

Bodégon Alejandro is a good spot for modern Basque cuisine in a sleek-yet-cozy cellar setting (€23 three-course fixed-price lunch, Tue-Sun 13:00-15:30 & 20:30-22:30 except closed Sun night, closed Mon, in Old Town on Calle Fermín Calbetón 4, tel. 943-427-158).

Bernardo Etxea is expert at serving up delicacies from the sea simply and deliciously. Friendly Chef Bernardo is particularly good at doing grilled seafood and meat dishes. This proper restaurant is popular with locals and celebrities alike. Look for happy celebrity diners including Meryl Streep, Oliver Stone, and Samuel L. Jackson on the "Wall of Fame." *Pintxos* are served at the bar (closed Wed evenings and Thu, Puerto 7, tel. 943-422-055).

Casa Urola is a must for San Sebastián gastronomy enthusiasts. Chef Pablo's updated versions of traditional Basque dishes even persuade other local chefs to eat here after finishing their shifts. Much of the exquisite menu changes seasonally. The peaceful, upstairs dining room has a contemporary elegance (reservations recommended). Without reservations, go downstairs—there are few tables, so most eat standing at the bar (€1.50-3.70 *pintxos*, €15-28 main courses, €7 desserts, *media ración*—half-portion— available for several dishes, extensive wine list; Wed-Mon 13:00-16:00 & 20:00-23:00, bar open until late, closed Tue; Fermín Calbetón 20, tel. 943-441-371, www.casaurolajatetxea.es).

Txuleta is tucked-away on a small plaza near Santa Maria Church. While the service can be hit or miss, this restaurant excels at grilled meats and seasonal *pintxos* that are worth the hefty price. Be adventurous and try the *kokotxas* (hake cheeks). The glass-enclosed terrace provides lots of seating (€2-3 *pintxos*, €8-16 *entrantes*—appetizers, €17-25 main courses, closed Mon evening and Tue, Plaza de la Trinidad 2, tel. 943-441-007, www.txuleta restaurante.com).

Seafood Along the Port: For seafood with a salty sailor's view, check out the half-dozen hardworking, local-feeling restaurants that line the harbor on the way to the aquarium. La Rampa is an upscale eatery, specializing in crab *(txangurro)* and lobster dishes and seafood *parillada* (€30-50 for dinner, closed Tue evenings, also closed Wed and Sun in winter, Paseo Muelle/Kaiko Pasealekua 26-27, tel. 943-421-652, www.restaurantelarampa.com). Also along here, locals like Sebastián (more traditional, closed Tue).

RESTAURANTS AND *PINTXO* BARS IN GROS

Bodega Donostiarra has been a San Sebastián institution since 1928. Locals flock here for sit-down meals with freshly made Spanish tortillas, meats of the grilled and cured varieties, and seafood. For a quick bite, head to their original, zinc bar for *pintxos* or a *sandwich completo* with tuna, onions, and anchovies (Sun-Thu 9:30-23:00, Fri-Sat 9:30-24:00, Calle Peña y Goñi 13, tel. 943-911-380).

Bar Bergara serves refined *pintxos* in a casually cool setting. Originally run by *chef-savante* Patxi Bergara, his nephews Monty and Esteban now continue the ethic of serving award-winning *pintxos* that are "eye-catching, original, and petite enough to eat in two bites." Cold snacks are artfully displayed on the bar, while *pintxos calientes* are made when ordered. Ask for an English menu (daily 9:30-16:00 & 18:00-24:00, to-go sandwiches available, General Artetxe 8, tel. 943-275-026).

Tedone is one of the few quality vegetarian options in this city of *gastronomía*. Hiding out on a tiny lane, this health-conscious eatery dishes up flavorful organic options that are truly Basque (Mon-Sat 12:45-15:30 & 20:30-23:00, closed Sun, Corta 10, tel. 943-273-561).

Thursday Night Party Scene: Every Thursday in Gros, university students and those who want to save some euros brave the masses for *pintxo-pote* (PEEN-cho POH-teh). Because of the increased popularity of gastronomy and *pintxos* in San Sebastián, locals, who often eat out regularly, want a good deal for food and drinks. Bars, particularly along **Calle Zabaleta** (between Gran Vía and Avenida Navarra) and parallel streets, offer a drink (usually beer or wine) and a basic *pintxo* for €2. It's basically a happy hour scene that spills out onto the streets. Just follow the crowds and remember that this isn't just sustenance, it's a social event (19:00-23:00).

PICNICS AND TAKEOUT

A picnic on the beach or atop Monte Urgull is a tempting option. You can assemble a bang-up spread at the **Bretxa Public Market** at Plaza de Sarriegi (described earlier).

Solbes, just across the street from the Bretxa Public Market, has a reputation as *the* gourmet deli store in the Old Town. There's a remarkable wine selection in the back cellar, plus high-quality cured meats and cheeses out front. Be sure to price fruits and veggies on the scale yourself to avoid confusion at checkout (Mon-Sat 9:00-20:30, Sun 9:00-14:30, Calle Aldamar 4, tel. 943-427-818).

Upscale **Barrenetxe** has an amazing array of breads, prepared foods, and some of the best desserts in town. You can also grab a coffee in the bar section. In business since 1699, their somewhat formal service is justified (daily 8:00-20:30, Plaza de Guipúzcoa 9, tel. 943-424-482).

BREAKFAST

If your hotel doesn't provide breakfast—or even if it does—consider one of these Old Town places. The first is a traditional stand-up bar; the second is a greasy spoon. If you're staying in Gros, consider Hogar Dulce Hogar.

Bar Gorriti, delightfully local, is packed with market workers and shoppers starting their day. You'll stand at the bar and choose a hot-off-the-grill *francesca jamón* omelet (fluffy mini-omelet sandwich topped with a slice of ham) and other goodies (€2 each). This and a good cup of coffee makes for a very Basque breakfast. By the time you get there for breakfast, many market workers will be taking their mid-morning break (daily, breakfast served 7:00-10:00, facing the side of the big white market building at San Juan 3, tel. 943-428-353).

Santa Lucía, a 1950s-style diner, is ideal for a cheap Old Town breakfast or *churros* break (*churros* are like deep-fried doughnut sticks that can be dipped in pudding-like hot chocolate). Photos of two dozen different breakfasts decorate the walls, and plates of fresh *churros* keep patrons happy. Grease is liberally applied to the grill...from a squeeze bottle (daily 8:30-21:30, Calle Puerto 6, tel. 943-425-019).

In Gros, **Hogar Dulce Hogar** (Home Sweet Home) is a solid breakfast option that serves other delightful sweet and savory treats throughout the day. If *torrija* (a decadently dense version of French toast) is on the menu, go for it. There's ample seating in this eatery where rustic meets hipster (Calle Bermingham 1 at Calle Zabaleta, tel. 943-246-681).

San Sebastián Connections

BY TRAIN
San Sebastián has two train stations: RENFE and Amara EuskoTren. The station you use depends on your destination.

RENFE Station: This station handles long-distance destinations within Spain (most of which require reservations). Connections include **Irún** (8/day, 25 minutes), **Hendaye,** France (4/day, 30 minutes; better connections on EuskoTren, described below), **Madrid** (4/day, 5.25-7.5 hours), **Burgos** (6/day, 3 hours), **León** (1/day, 5 hours), **Pamplona** (2/day, 1.75 hours), **Salamanca** (5/day, 6 hours), **Barcelona** (2/day, 6 hours), and **Santiago de Compostela** (1-2/day direct, 10.5 hours).

Amara EuskoTren Station: If you're going into France, take the regional Topo train (which leaves from the Amara EuskoTren Station) over the French border into **Hendaye** (usually 4/hour Mon-Fri, 2/hour Sat-Sun, 35 minutes). From Hendaye, connect to France's SNCF network (www.sncf.com), where connections include **Paris** (6/day direct, 5.5-6 hours; 12-hour night train, weekends only off-season, reservations required). Unfortunately, San Sebastián's EuskoTren Station doesn't have information on Paris-bound trains from Hendaye. EuskoTren tickets to Hendaye must be used within two hours of purchase (or else they expire).

Also leaving from San Sebastián's Amara EuskoTren Station

are slow regional trains to destinations in Spain's Basque region, including **Bilbao** (hourly, 2.5 hours—the bus is faster, EuskoTren info: tel. 902-543-210, www.euskotren.es). Although the train ride from San Sebastián to Bilbao takes twice as long as the bus, it passes through more interesting countryside. The Basque Country shows off its trademark green and gray: lush green vegetation and gray clouds. It's an odd mix of heavy industrial factories, small homegrown veggie gardens, streams, and every kind of livestock you can imagine.

BY BUS

San Sebastián's "bus station," called Amara (for the neighborhood), is a congregation of bus parking spots next to the big Hotel Amara Plaza, at Plaza Pío XII (on the river, four blocks south of EuskoTren Station; take bus #21, #26, or #28 from Boulevard). Some schedules are posted at various stops, but confirm departure times. You must buy your tickets in advance at the bus companies, with offices on either side of the block north of the station area (toward downtown, along Avenida de Sancho el Sabio and Paseo de Vízcaya). Bus tickets are not available from the driver. The Pesa office, which serves St-Jean-de-Luz and Bilbao, is located at Avenida de Sancho el Sabio 33 (Mon-Fri 6:10-22:00, Sat-Sun 8:00-20:30, tel. 902-101-210, www.pesa.net). The Alsa office—which serves Madrid, Burgos, and León—is just beyond Pesa at Sancho el Sabio 31 and has handy multilingual kiosks (daily 6:45-21:00, tel. 902-422-242, www.alsa.es). Conda—which serves Pamplona and Bayonne—shares an office with Alsa (tel. 943-461-064, www.conda.es). The Vibasa office—which serves Burgos, Pamplona, and Barcelona—is on the other side of the block along the river, at Calle Vízcaya 15 (closed 13:30-15:00, tel. 902-101-363, www.vibasa.com).

From San Sebastián, buses go to **Bilbao** (2/hour, hourly on weekends, 6:30-22:00, 1.25 hours, get ticket from Pesa office, departs from Amara; morning buses fill with tourists, commuters, and students, so consider buying your ticket the day before; once in Bilbao, buses leave you at Termibús stop with easy tram connections to the Guggenheim modern-art museum); **Bilbao Airport** (a Pesa bus leaves directly from Plaza Pío XII, hourly, 1.25 hours, get tickets from Pesa office), **Pamplona** (8-10/day, 1 hour, Conda office), **León** (1/day, 6 hours, Alsa office), **Madrid** (8/day, 6 hours direct, otherwise 7 hours; a few departures direct to Madrid's Barajas Airport, 5.25 hours; Alsa office), **Burgos** (7/day, 2-3 hours, Alsa or Vibasa office), and **Barcelona** (2/day and 1 at night, 7 hours, Vibasa office).

To visit **Hondarribia** (described next), you can catch bus #E21 or #E23 much closer to the center at Plaza de Gipuzkoa (1 block south of TI; about 3/hour, 35 minutes, #E21 goes to airport en route to Hondarribia).

Buses to French Basque Country: A bus goes from San Sebastián's Amara bus station to **St-Jean-de-Luz** (Mon-Sat only, 2/day at 9:00 and 14:30, none on Sun, 1 hour, return trips likely at 12:45 and 19:15, only 1/week off-season, get ticket from Pesa office), then continues directly to **Biarritz** (1.25 hours from San Sebastián) and **Bayonne** (1.5 hours from San Sebastián).

Fuenterrabía / Hondarribia

For a taste of small-town *País Vasco,* dip into this enchanting, seldom-visited town. It's more commonly known by its Euskara

name, Hondarribia, than the Spanish version, Fuenterrabía. Much smaller and easier to manage than San Sebastián, and also closer to France (across the picturesque Bay of Txingudi from Hendaye), Hondarribia allows travelers a stress-free opportunity to enjoy Basque culture. While it's easy to think of this as a border town (between France and Spain), culturally it's in the middle of the Basque Country.

The town comes in two parts: the lower port town and the historic, balcony-lined streets of the hilly and walled upper town. The upper town, which feels quite manicured, is a delightful place to poke around if you have time. The main square is fronted by Charles V's austere, oddly squat castle (now a parador inn). You can follow the TI's self-guided tour of the Old Town (English brochure available) or just lose yourself within the walls to discover hidden plazas and former royal residences. In the modern lower town, straight shopping streets serve a local clientele, and a pleasant walkway takes strollers along the beach.

Tourist Information: There are two TIs. One is located on the main square, Plaza de Armas, across from the parador; the other is at Minatera 9, near the port (both July-Sept daily 10:30-13:30 & 15:30-20:00; shorter hours and closed Mon Oct-June; tel. 943-645-458, www.bidasoaturismo.com).

Arrival in Hondarribia: For some beach time, drivers can use the metered parking by the port (marked with blue lines, pre-pay for parking at machine). If you're here during the week off-season, the giant lot on the beach is free. Drivers who only want to explore the Old Town should follow signs to *Casco Viejo* and park at the free, tree-lined lot immediately across from the gate in the city wall; look for its giant coat-of-arms (Alameda de Daniel Vázquez Díaz). Buses into town stop near the main square.

Sleeping in Hondarribia: Accommodations are pricey here, but it's a nice small-town alternative to San Sebastián. **$$$** Parador El Emperador, with 34 rooms housed in a former imperial fortress, is the town's splurge. Tourists are allowed to have sangria in the *muy* cool bar, though the terraces are for guests only (Sb-€188, Db-€248, Db with view-€270, includes breakfast, elevator, Wi-Fi, Plaza de Armas 14, tel. 943-645-500, www.parador.es, hondarribia@parador.es). **$$** Hotel San Nikolas, facing the parador from across the square, offers a more affordable alternative, with 17 nicely appointed rooms (many with views) above a local café (Sb-€41-61, Db-€66-83, Db with sea view-€83-99, higher price is for mid-July-mid-Sept, can be even cheaper Mon-Thu off-season, elevator, Wi-Fi, Plaza de Armas 6, tel. 943-644-278, www.hotelsannikolas.es, info@hotelsannikolas.es).

Hondarribia Connections: From Hondarribia, buses go to **San Sebastián**'s Plaza de Gipuzkoa (about 3/hour, 35 minutes on express buses #E23 or #E21, departs near main square—#E21 also stops at airport; or twice as long on local public buses #E26 and night bus #E77) and to **Irún** near the French border (2/hour, 20 minutes, buses #E25 and night bus #E77). A **boat** goes to **Hendaye** (4/hour in summer, 2/hour off-season, 10 minutes, runs about 11:00-19:00 or until dark).

Route Tips for Drivers: Leaving San Sebastián passing Zurriola Beach in Gros, first follow signs to *Irún/Frantzia;* signs for *Hondarribia* appear after about 20 minutes. If continuing on to St-Jean-de-Luz, signs to *Baiona* lead back to the main highway and the French border. Have coins ready to chuck into the automatic toll booth.

The Bay of Biscay

Between the two Spanish Basque cities of San Sebastián and Bilbao is a beautiful countryside of rolling green hills and a scenic, jagged

coastline that looks almost Celtic. Aside from a scenic joyride, this area merits a visit for the cute fishing and resort town of Lekeitio.

ROUTE TIPS FOR DRIVERS

San Sebastián and Bilbao are connected in about an hour and a quarter by the A-8 toll road. While speedy and scenic, this route is nothing compared to some of the free, but slower, back roads with lots of twists and turns that connect the two towns.

If side-tripping from San Sebastián to Bilbao, you can drive directly there on A-8 in the morning. But coming home to San Sebastián, consider this more scenic route: Take A-8 until the turnoff for Guernica (look for *Amorebieta/Gernika-Lumo* sign), then head up into the hills on BI-635. After visiting Guernica, follow signs along the very twisty BI-2238 road to Lekeitio (about 40 minutes). Leave Lekeitio on the road just above the beach; after crossing the bridge, take the left fork and follow BI-3438 to Markina/Ondarroa (with a striking modern bridge and nice views back into the steep town; follow *portua* signs for free 30-minute parking at the port). Continue to Mutriku and Deba as you hug the coastline east toward San Sebastián. There's a good photo-op pullout as you climb along the coast just after Deba. Soon after, you'll have two opportunities to get on the A-8 (blue signs) for a quicker approach to San Sebastián; but if you've enjoyed the scenery so far, stick with the coastal road (white signs, N-634) through Zumaia and Getaria, rejoining the expressway at the high-class resort town of Zarautz.

LEQUEITIO/LEKEITIO

More commonly known by its Euskara name, Lekeitio (leh-KAY-tee-oh)—rather than the Spanish version, Lequeitio—this small

fishing port has an idyllic harbor and a fine beach. It's just over an hour by bus from Bilbao and an easy stop for drivers, and is protected from the Bay of Biscay by a sand spit that leads to the lush and rugged little San Nicolás Island. Hake boats fly their Basque flags, and proud Basque locals black out the Spanish translations on street signs.

Lekeitio is a teeming resort during July and August (when its population of 7,000 triples as big-city Basque folks move into their vacation condos). Isolated from the modern rat race by its location down a long, windy little road, it's a backwater fishing village the rest of the year.

Sights here are humble, though the 15th-century St. Mary's Parish Church is a good example of Basque Gothic, with an impressive altarpiece. The town's back lanes are reminiscent of old days when fishing was the only industry. Fisherwomen sell their husbands' catches each morning along the port. The golden crescent beach is as inviting as the sandbar, which—at low tide—challenges you to join the seagulls out on San Nicolás Island.

The best beach in the area for surfers and sun lovers is Playas Laga (follow signs off the road from Bilbao to Lekeitio). Relatively uncrowded, it's popular with body-boarders.

Getting There: Buses connect Lekeitio with **Bilbao** (hourly, 1.25 hours; same bus stops at **Guernica,** 40 minutes) and **San Sebastián** (4/day Mon-Fri, 2/day Sat-Sun, 1.25 hours). But this destination is most logical for those with a car. Drivers can park most easily in the lot near the bus station. Exit the station left, walk along the road, then take the first right (down the steep, cobbled street) to reach the harbor. There is no luggage storage in town.

Tourist Information: The TI faces the fish market next to the harbor (July-Aug daily 10:00-14:00 & 16:00-20:00; shorter hours and closed Mon Sept-June; tel. 946-844-017, www.lekeitio.org).

Sleeping in Lekeitio: A few steps from the harbor, **$$ Hotel Aisia Lekeitio** is the obvious best bet for your beach-town break. Empress Zita lived here in exile after her Habsburg family lost World War I and was booted from Vienna. Zita's mansion burned down, but this 1930s rebuild still has an aristocratic belle époque charm, with solid classy furniture in 42 spacious rooms and an elegant spa in the basement (Sb-€60-77, Db-€70-101, Db suite-€103-134, views—ask for *vistas del mar*—are worth it, prices can be higher July-Aug and Sat all year, extra bed-€25, breakfast-€10, elevator, Wi-Fi, free parking, view restaurant, Santa Elena Etorbidea, tel. 946-842-655, www.aisiahoteles.com, lekeitio@aisiahoteles.com). The hotel also has a thermal seawater pool, a Jacuzzi, and a full-service spa (all available at reasonable prices).

Eating in Lekeitio: Although it's sleepy off-season, the harbor promenade is made-to-order in summer for a slow meal or a tapas crawl. **Restaurante Kaia** offers a mostly seafood menu, with a €15 fixed-priced lunch (Tue-Sat lunch and dinner, Sun dinner only, closed Mon, on the harbor at Txatxo Kaia 5, tel. 946-840-284).

Guernica / Gernika

The workaday market town of Guernica (GEHR-nee-kah) is near and dear to Basques and pacifists alike. This is the site of the Gernikako Arbola—the oak tree of Gernika, which marked the assembly point where the regional Basque leaders, the Lords of Bizkaia, met through the ages to assert their people's freedom. Long the symbolic heart of Basque separatism, it was also a natural target for Franco (and Hitler) in the Spanish Civil War—result-

ing in an infamous bombing raid that left the town in ruins (see "The Bombing of Guernica" sidebar), as immortalized by Picasso in his epic work *Guernica*.

Today's Guernica, rebuilt after being bombed flat in 1937 and nothing special at first glance, holds some of the Basque Country's more compelling museums. And Basque bigwigs have reclaimed the town as a meeting point—they still elect their figurehead leader on that same ancient site under the oak tree.

Orientation to Guernica

Guernica is small (about 17,000 inhabitants) and compact, focused on its large market hall (Monday market 9:00-14:00).

Tourist Information: The TI is in the town center (Mon-Sat 10:00-14:00 & 16:00-19:00, Sun 10:00-14:00, longer hours in summer, Artekalea 8, tel. 946-255-892, www.gernika-lumo.net). Pick up the free, good town map. If you'll be visiting both the Peace Museum and the Basque Country Museum, buy the €4.50 combo-ticket here.

Arrival in Guernica: Drivers will find a handy parking lot near the train tracks at the end of town. Buses drop off passengers along the main road skirting the town center. No matter where you enter, the TI is well signed (look for yellow *i* signs)—head there first to get your bearings.

Sights in Guernica

I've listed Guernica's sights in the order of a handy sightseeing loop from the TI.
• *Exit the TI to the left, cross the street, and walk up the left side of the square, where you'll find the...*

▲Gernika Peace Museum

Because of the brutality of the Guernica bombing, and the powerful Picasso painting that documented the atrocities of war, the name "Guernica" has become synonymous with pacifism. This thoughtfully presented exhibit has taken a great tragedy of 20th-century history and turned it into a compelling cry for peace in our time.

Cost and Hours: €5, Tue-Sat 10:00-19:00, Sun 10:00-14:00, closed Mon, Foru Plaza 1, tel. 946-270-213, www.peacemuseum guernica.org.

Visiting the Museum: Borrow the English translations at the entry, request an English showing of the movie upstairs, and head up through the two-floor exhibit. The first floor begins by considering different ways of defining "peace." You'll then enter an apartment and hear a local woman, Begoña, describe her typical Guernica life in the 1930s...until the bombs dropped (a mirror effect shows you the devastating aftermath). You'll exit through the rubble into an exhibit about the town's history, with a special emphasis on the bombing. Finally, a 10-minute movie shows grainy footage of the destruction, and ends with a collage of peaceful reconciliations in recent history—in Ireland, South Africa, Guatemala, Australia, and Berlin. On the second floor, Picasso's famous painting is superimposed on three transparent panels to highlight different themes. The exhibit concludes with a survey of the recent history of conflicts in the Basque Country.

• *Continue uphill to the big church. At the road above the church, you can turn right and walk a block and a half to find an underwhelming tile replica of* **Picasso's** **Guernica** *(left-hand side of the street). Or you can head left to find the next two attractions.*

▲Basque Country Museum (Euskal Herria Museoa)

This well-presented exhibit offers a good overview of Basque culture and history. Start in the ground-floor theater (Room 4) and see the overview video (request English). Follow the suggested route and climb chronologically up through Basque history, with the necessary help of an included audioguide. You'll find exhibits about traditional Basque architecture and landscape, lots of antique maps, and a region-by-region rundown of the Basque Country's seven territories. One interesting map shows Basque emigration over the centuries—including to the US. The top floor is the most engaging, highlighting Basque culture: sports, dances, cuisine, myths and legends, music, and language, plus a wrap-around movie featuring images of a proud people living the Basque lifestyle. For a breath of fresh air, step out back into the **Peoples of Europe Park** and enjoy a peaceful respite.

Cost and Hours: €3, free on Sat, includes audioguide—except on Sat, open Tue-Sat 10:00-14:00 & 16:00-19:00, Sun 10:30-14:00, closed Mon, Allendesalazar 5, tel. 946-255-451.

▲▲Gernika Assembly House and Oak Tree

In the Middle Ages, the meeting point for the Basque general assembly was under the old oak tree on the gentle hillside above Guernica. The tradition continues today, as the tree stands at the center of a modest but interesting complex celebrating Basque culture and self-government.

Cost and Hours: Free, daily 10:00-14:00 & 16:00-18:00, June-Sept until 19:00, on Allendesalazar, tel. 946-251-138.

Visiting the Assembly House: As you enter the grounds past the guard hut, on the right you'll see an **old tree trunk** in the small colonnade dating from the 1700s. Basque traditions have lived much, much longer than a single tree's life span. When one dies, it's replaced with a new one. This is the oldest surviving trunk.

The Bombing of Guernica

During the civil war, Guernica was the site of one of history's most reviled wartime acts.

Monday, April 26, 1937 was market day, when the town was filled with farmers and peasants from the countryside selling their wares. At about 16:40 in the afternoon, a German warplane appeared ominously on the horizon, and proceeded to bomb bridges and roads surrounding the town. Soon after, more planes arrived. Three hours of relentless saturation bombing followed, as the German and Italian air forces pummeled the city with incendiary firebombs. People running through the streets or along the green hillsides were strafed with machine-gun fire. As the sun fell low in the sky and the planes finally left, hundreds—or possibly thousands—had been killed, and many more wounded. (Because Guernica was filled with refugees from other besieged towns, nobody is sure how many perished.)

Hearing word of the attack in Paris, Pablo Picasso—who had been commissioned to paint a mural for the 1937 world's fair—was devastated at the news of what had gone on in Guernica. Inspired, he painted what many consider the greatest antiwar work of art, ever.

Why did the bombings happen? Reportedly, Adolf Hitler wanted an opportunity to try out his new saturation-bombing attack strategy. Spanish dictator Francisco Franco, who was fed up with the independence-minded Basques, offered up their historic capital as a candidate for the experiment.

There's no doubt that Guernica, a gateway to Bilbao, was strategically located. And yet, a small munitions factory that supplied anti-Franco forces with pistols oddly wasn't hit by the bombing. Historians believe most of the targets here were far from strategic. Why attack so mercilessly, during the daytime, on market day, when innocent casualties would be maximized? Like the famous silent scream of Picasso's *Guernica* mother, this question haunts pacifists everywhere to this day.

The exhibit has four parts: a stained-glass window room, the oak-tree courtyard, the assembly chamber, and a basement theater (request the 10-minute video in English that extols the virtues and beauties of the Basque Country).

Inside the main building, request a copy of the English-language brochure that describes in detail the importance of this site. First find the impressive **stained-glass window room.** The computer video here gives a good six-minute overview of the exhibit (plays in English when you click). The gorgeous stained-glass ceiling is rife with Basque symbolism. The elderly leader stands under the oak holding a book with the "Old Law" *(Lege Zarra)*, which are the laws by which the Basques lived for centuries. Below him

are groups representing the three traditional career groups of this industrious people: sailors and fishermen; miners and steelworkers; and farmers. Behind them all is a classic Basque landscape: On the left is the sea, and on the right are rolling green hills dotted with red-and-white homes. Small, square panels around the large window represent all the important towns in the region, with Guernica's oak tree easy to pinpoint.

Out back, a Greek-style tribune surrounds the fateful **oak tree.** This little fella is from 2005, planted here when the earlier one "finished out its life cycle" after standing here for nearly a century and a half. This tree is a descendant of that one, and possibly of all the trees here since ancient times. This location is where Basque leaders have met in solidarity across the centuries.

In the Middle Ages, after Basque lands became part of Castile, Castilian kings came here to pledge respect to the old Basque laws. When Basque independence came under fire in the 19th century, patriots rallied by singing a song about this tree ("Ancient and holy symbol / Let thy fruit fall worldwide / While we gaze in adoration / Upon thee, our blessed tree"). After the 1937 bombing, in which this tree's predecessor was miraculously unscathed, hundreds of survivors sought refuge under its branches. Today, although official representatives in the Spanish government are elected at the polls, the Basques choose their figurehead leader, the Lehendakari ("First One"), in this same spot.

Step back inside and enter the **assembly chamber**—like a mini-parliament for the region of Bizkaia ("Vízcaya" in Spanish, "Biscay" in English; one of the seven Basque territories). Notice the holy water and the altar—a sign that there's no separation of church and state in Basque politics. The large paintings above the doors show the swearing of allegiance to the Old Law. Portraits of 26 former Lords of Bizkaia maintain a watchful eye over the current assembly's decisions.

• *Exiting the grounds of the Assembly House, walk back to the front of the Basque Country Museum, and take the stairs on your right down to Pasealekua Square. At the bottom of the stairs, pop into a café (on your left) known to locals as the...*

Bar de los Jubilados (Old Bomb Shelter)

This unmarked café, part of the retirement community center housed in the same building, is a good place for a quick coffee and snack—but it's main claim to fame is that it was a bomb shelter during the 1937 bombing. Ask the bartender, *¿Dónde está el t...*

por favor? You'll be directed towards the women's restroom (gentlemen, don't worry, you can go, too). Walk down the hall, turn right into the women's restroom, and go past the stalls into a small, cold, two-part room. While not much to look at these days, imagine dozens of panicked people scrambling to take shelter here, hoping and praying that they would live through the devastating aerial attack (daily 10:30-21:30, Pasealekua Square).

Guernica Connections

Guernica is well connected to **Bilbao** (2 trains/hour, 50 minutes, arrive at Bilbao's Atxuri Station; also 4 buses/hour, 40 minutes) and to **Lekeitio** (hourly buses, 40 minutes). Connections are sparser on weekends. The easiest way to connect to San Sebastián is via Bilbao, though you can also get there on the slow "Topo" EuskoTren train (transfer in Lemoa, about 3-4 hours).

Bilbao / Bilbo

In recent years, Bilbao (bil-BOW, rhymes with "cow") has seen a transformation like no other Spanish city. Entire sectors of the industrial city's long-depressed port have been cleared away to allow construction of a new convention center and the stunning Guggenheim Museum.

Bilbao retains less and less of its grim industrial past...and looks toward an exciting new future. But some of the grime hangs on. The city mingles beautiful but crumbling old buildings; eyesore high-rise apartment blocks; brand-new super-modern additions to the skyline (such as the Guggenheim and its neighbor, the 40-story Iberdrola Tower); and, scattered in the lush green hillsides all around the horizon, typical whitewashed Basque homes with red roofs. Bilbao enjoys a vitality and well-worn charm befitting its status as a regional capital of culture and industry.

PLANNING YOUR TIME

For most visitors, the Guggenheim is the main draw (and many could spend the entire day there). But with a little more time, it's also worth hopping on a tram to explore the atmospheric Old Town (Casco Viejo). With extra time, take the Mount Artxanda funicular for a breathtaking overview of the entire area. Don't bother coming to Bilbao on Monday, when virtually all its museums—including the almighty Guggenheim—are closed (except in ᵣ ᵗly-Aug).

Orientation to Bilbao

When you're in the center, Bilbao feels smaller than its population of 350,000. The city, nestled amidst green hillsides, hugs the

Bilbao River as it curves through town. The Guggenheim is more or less centrally located near the top of that curve; the bus station is to the west; the Old Town (Casco Viejo) and train stations are to the east; and a super-convenient and fun-to-ride green tram called the EuskoTran ties it all together.

TOURIST INFORMATION

Bilbao's handiest TI is near the Guggenheim. Pick up a city map and the bimonthly *Bilbao Guide*. If you're interested in something beyond the Guggenheim, ask about their city walking tours in English (€4.50, Sat-Sun year-round, more often in summer) or their various self-guided walks focusing on particular neighborhoods, bridges, architecture, and the "Green Belt"—the hilly forest preserve surrounding the city. Grab the Bilbao museums brochure, describing museums dedicated to everything from bullfighting and seafaring to sports and Holy Week processionals (daily 10:00-19:00, Sun until 15:00 in off-season; Alameda Mazarredo 66, tel. 944-795-760, www.bilbaoturismo.net).

A second convenient city TI is housed in a former bank next to the RENFE station at Plaza Circular; look for the red *i* sign above the door (daily 9:00-21:00). The Basque Country regional TI office at the airport can help you with information about Bilbao and the entire region (daily 10:00-14:00 & 15:00-19:00, tel. 944-031-444, www.tourism.euskadi.net).

Sightseeing Card: The **Bilbao Card** is sold at TIs and provides unlimited use of the metro, tram, funicular, and Bilbobus urban buses. It also entitles you to free TI walking tours and discounts on city museums—except the Guggenheim (€6/1 day, €10/2 days).

ARRIVAL IN BILBAO

Most travelers—whether arriving by train, bus, or car—will want to go straight to the Guggenheim. Thanks to a perfectly planned tram system (EuskoTran), this couldn't be easier. From any point of entry, simply buy a €1.50 single-ride

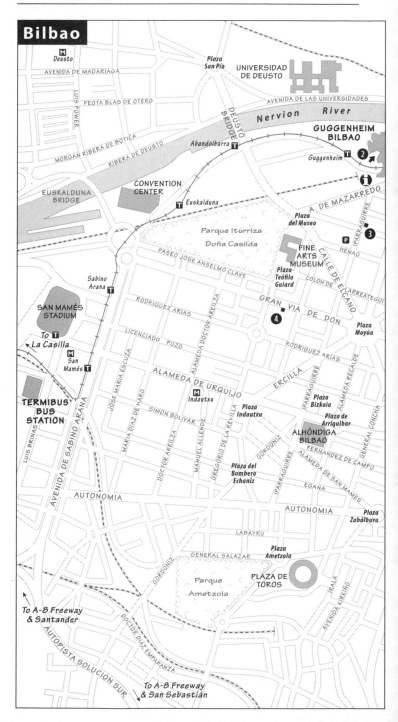

Bilbao

Deusto

AVENIDA DE MADARIAGA

LUIS POWER

PEOTA BLAS DE OTERO

Plaza San Pío

UNIVERSIDAD DE DEUSTO

AVENIDA DE LAS UNIVERSIDADES

MORGAN RIBERA DE BOTICA

RIBERA DE DEUSTO

DEUSTO BRIDGE

Nervion   River

Abandoibarra

GUGGENHEIM BILBAO

Guggenheim   ②

EUSKALDUNA BRIDGE

CONVENTION CENTER

Euskalduna

A DE MAZARREDO

❸

Plaza del Museo

IPARRAGUIRRE

HENAO

Parque Iturriza Doña Casilda

PASEO JOSE ANSELMO CLAVE

FINE ARTS MUSEUM

P

Sabino Arana

Plaza Teófilo Guiard

COLON DE LA

ARREATEGUI

SAN MAMÉS STADIUM

RODRIGUEZ ARIAS

GRAN   VIA   DE DON

❹

To La Casilla

San Mamés

LICENCIADO   POZO

ALAMEDA DOCTOR AREILZA

Plaza Moyúa

RODRIGUEZ ARIAS

ERCILLA

IPARRAGUIRRE

ALAMEDA RECALDE

TERMIBUS BUS STATION

AVENIDA DE SABINO ARANA

JOSE MARIA ESCUZA

ALAMEDA DE URQUIJO

Indautxu

Plaza Indautxu

Plaza Bizkaia

GENERAL CONCHA

LUIS BRIÑAS

MARIA DIAZ DE HARO

DOCTOR AREILZA

SIMON BOLIVAR

MANUEL ALLENDE

GREGORIO DE LA REVILLA

GORDONIZ

Plaza de Arriquibar

ALHÓNDIGA BILBAO

FERNANDEZ DE CAMPO

ALAMEDA DE SAN MAMES

IPARRAGUIRRE

EGANA

AUTONOMIA

Plaza del Bombero Echaniz

AUTONOMIA

Plaza Zabálburu

LABAYRU

GENERAL SALAZAR

Plaza Ametzola

GORDONIZ

DOCTOR DIAZ EMPARANZA

Parque Ametzola

PLAZA DE TOROS

IRALA

AVENIDA KIRIKIÑO

To A-8 Freeway & Santander

AUTOPISTA SOLUCION SUR

To A-8 Freeway & San Sebastián

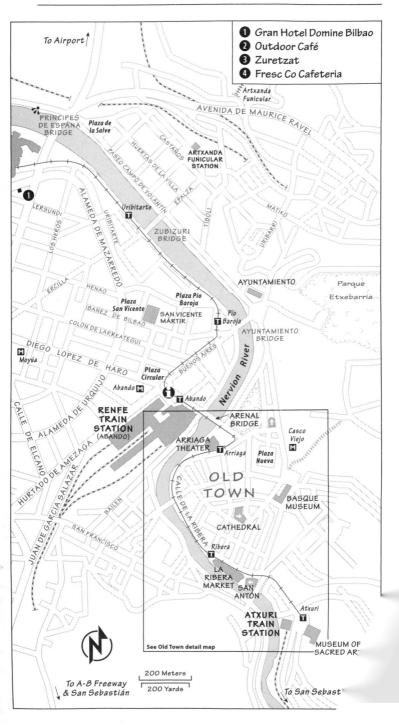

1. Gran Hotel Domine Bilbao
2. Outdoor Café
3. Zuretzat
4. Fresc Co Cafeteria

To Airport

PRINCIPES DE ESPAÑA BRIDGE

Plaza de la Salve

AVENIDA DE MAURICE RAVEL

Artxanda Funicular

ARTXANDA FUNICULAR STATION

LERSUNDI

LOS HEROS

ALAMEDA DE MAZARREDO

PASEO CAMPO DE VOLANTÍN

URIBITARTE

Uribitarte

ZUBIZURI BRIDGE

HUERTAS DE LA VILLA

CASTAÑOS

EPALZA

TÍBOLI

MATIKO

URIBARRI

AYUNTAMIENTO

Parque Etxebarria

ERCILLA

HENAO

IBAÑEZ DE BILBAO

COLON DE LARREATEGUI

Plaza San Vicente

SAN VICENTE MÁRTIR

Plaza Pío Baroja

Pío Baroja

AYUNTAMIENTO BRIDGE

DIEGO LOPEZ DE HARO

Moyúa

ALAMEDA DE URQUIJO

Plaza Circular

Abando

BUENOS AIRES

Abando

Nervion River

ARENAL BRIDGE

Casco Viejo

CALLE DE ELCANO

HURTADO DE AMEZAGA

JUAN DE GARCIA SALAZAR

RENFE TRAIN STATION (ABANDO)

ARRIAGA THEATER

Arriaga

Plaza Nueva

OLD TOWN

BASQUE MUSEUM

BAILEN

SAN FRANCISCO

CALLE DE LA RIBERA

CATHEDRAL

Ribera

LA RIBERA MARKET

SAN ANTÓN

ATXURI TRAIN STATION

Atxuri

MUSEUM OF SACRED ART

See Old Town detail map

To A-8 Freeway & San Sebastián

200 Meters
200 Yards

To San Sebast'

ticket at a user-friendly green machine (€4.20 for an all-day pass), hop on a green-and-gray tram, enjoy the Muzak, and head for the Guggenheim stop (there's only one line, trams come every 10-15 minutes, tel. 902-543-210, www.euskotren.es—choose "Tranvía Bilbao"). When you buy your ticket, validate it immediately at the machine (follow the red arrow), since you can't do it once on board. If you get lost, ask: *"¿Dónde está el Guggenheim?"* (DOHN-deh eh-STAH el "Guggenheim"). Note that the only luggage storage in town is at the Termibús Station (not at either train station). Don't confuse the green tram (Eusko*Tran*) with the slow, scenic, blue train to San Sebastián (Eusko*Tren*).

By Train: Bilbao's **RENFE station** (serving most of Spain) is on the river in central Bilbao. The train station is on top of a small shopping mall (a Europcar rental office is near the train-station ticket office, tel. 944-239-390). To reach the tram to the Guggenheim, descend into the stores. Leave from the exit marked *Hurtado de Amézaga*, and go right to find the BBK bank. Enter, find the *Automatikoa* door on the right, and buy your ticket at the green machine marked *Abando* (the machine is mixed in with a bunch of ATMs). Leave the bank and continue right around the corner. Validate your ticket at the machines at the tram stop before boarding the tram (direction: La Casilla).

Trains coming from San Sebastián arrive at the riverside **Atxuri Station,** southeast of the museum. From here the tram (direction: La Casilla) follows the river to the Guggenheim stop.

By Bus: Buses stop at the **Termibús Station** on the western edge of downtown, about a mile southwest of the Guggenheim. Don't expect a real building—it's just a covered parking lot with small portables. The tram (San Mamés Station) is on the road just below the station—look for the steel *CTB* sign or follow the *Tran* signs. Buy and validate a ticket at the machine, and hop on the tram (direction: Atxuri) to the Guggenheim or Old Town.

By Plane: Bilbao's compact, modern, user-friendly airport (airport code: BIO) is about six miles north of downtown. Everything branches off the light-and-air-filled main hall, designed by prominent architect Santiago Calatrava. The handy Bizkaibus (#3247) takes you directly to the city center—look for a green sign outside the far right exit of the terminal (€1.40, pay driver, daily 6:00-24:00, 2/hour, 20-minute trip, makes three stops downtown—the first one is closest to the Guggenheim—before ⌐ding at the Termibús Station). A taxi into town costs about €25.

get to San Sebastián, you can take a direct bus from Bilbao ⌐ort (€17.50, pay driver, runs hourly, 1.25 hours, drops off at ⌐ Pío XII in San Sebastián, www.pesa.net). A taxi directly to ⌐bastián will run you €150.

Car: A big underground parking garage is near the

museum; if you have a car, park it here and use the tram. From the freeway, take the exit marked *Centro* (with bull's-eye symbol), follow signs to *Guggenheim* (you'll see the museum), and look for the big *P* that marks the garage.

HELPFUL HINTS

Baggage Storage: The Termibús Station on the west side of the city is your best option (lockers: €1/bag, use tokens from nearby machine; desk: €2/bag, Mon-Fri 7:00-22:00, Sat-Sun 8:00-21:00, Gurtubay 1, tel. 944-395-077).

Laundry: The self-service **Lavandería Autoservicio Adei** is handy for visitors staying in the Old Town. You don't even have to buy detergent—it's already dispensed in the machines (small load-€6, big load-€11, dryer-€1/10 minutes; daily 8:00-22:00, Ribera 9, mobile 665-710-082).

Tours in Bilbao

Walking Tours

Bilbao Walking Tours offers 1.5-hour tours on Saturdays and Sundays (more often in summer): an Old Town tour (starts at the Plaza Circular TI at 10:00), and a modern-city tour showing the city's history since the 19th century (starts at the Guggenheim TI at 12:00). Tours are in Spanish and English, and you must call ahead to reserve (€4.50, tel. 944-795-760, www.bilbao.net/bilbao turismo, informacion@bilbaoturismo.bilbao.net).

Tram Tour

Riding the EuskoTran round-trip between the Atxuri and Euskalduna stops is a great way to see the city's oldest and newest neighborhoods, especially on rainy days. For more on this tram, see "Arrival in Bilbao," earlier.

Bus Tour

The TI runs a decent hop-on, hop-off bus tour around the city. The hour-long trip picks up on the hour outside the Guggenheim TI, and has stops in the Old Town and across the river (€14, ticket valid 24 hours, buy at TI or from driver; July-Aug daily 11:00-18:00, April-June and Sept-Dec shorter hours and closed Tue, Jan-March Sat-Sun only; tel. 696-429-848, www.busturistikoa.com).

Boat Tour

For a different view of the city, try the **Bilboats** one-hour tour along the river, offering plenty of architectural Kodak moments. The tour begins near Ayuntamiento Bridge (€12, daily in spring and summer at 13:00, 16:00, 17:30, and 19:00, fewer departures off-season; reserve ahead, as trips are canceled if less than 10 people buy tickets; tram stop: Pío Baroja, Metro stop: Abando; Plaza de Pío Baroja, tel. 946-424-157, www.bilboats.com). For hardcore sailors, a two-hour weekend version goes all the way into the Bay of Biscay (€17, leaves at 10:30).

Local Guide

Knowledgeable Bilbao resident and licensed guide **Iratxe Muñoz** offers tours of the city, including the Guggenheim and the Basque region (rates vary, mobile 607-778-072, www.apite.eu/iratxemunoz, iratxe.m@apite.eu).

Sights in Bilbao

▲▲▲GUGGENHEIM BILBAO

Although the collection of art in this museum is no better than those in Europe's other great modern-art museums, the build-

ing itself—designed by Frank Gehry and opened in 1997— is reason enough for many travelers to happily splice Bilbao into their itineraries. Even if you're not turned on by contemporary art, the Guggenheim is a must-see experience. Its 20 galleries, on three floors, are full of surprises, and it's well worth the entry fee just to appreciate the museum's structural design, which is a masterpiece in itself.

Cost and Hours: €13; July-Aug daily 10:00-20:00; Sept-June Tue-Sun 10:00-20:00, closed Mon; same-day re-entry allowed—get wristband on your way out; café, no photos inside galleries, tram stop: Guggenheim, Metro stop: Moyúa, Avenida Abandoibarra 2, tel. 944-359-080, www.guggenheim-bilbao.es.

Tours: A free and excellent audioguide is included in your entry. Free, one-hour guided tours in Spanish generally run once a day at 17:00, possibly more in summer. Show up at least 30 minutes early to put your name on the list at the information desk (to the left as you enter). Guided tours in English are available only by advance reservation and with a fee (€95 for up to 20 people).

Background: Frank Gehry's groundbreaking triumph offers a fascinating look at 21st-century architecture. Using cutting-edge technologies, unusual materials, and daring forms, he created a piece of sculpture that smoothly integrates with its environment and serves as the perfect stage for some of today's best art. Clad in limestone and titanium, the building connects the city with its river. Gehry meshed many visions. To him, the building's multiple forms jostle like a loose crate of bottles. The building is inspired by a silvery fish...and also evokes wind-filled sails heading out to sea. Gehry keeps returning to his fish motif, reminding visitors that, as a boy, he was inspired by carp...even taking them into the bathtub with him.

✓ **Self-Guided Tour:** The audioguide will lead you room-by-room through the collection, but this information will get you started.

Guarding the main entrance is artist Jeff Koons' 42-foot-tall **West Highland Terrier.** Its 60,000 plants and flowers, which blossom in concert, grow through steel mesh. A joyful structure, it brings viewers back to their childhood—perhaps evoking humankind's relationship to God—or maybe it's just another notorious Koons hoax. One thing is clear: It answers to "Puppy." Although the sculpture was originally intended to be temporary, the people of Bilbao fell in love with *Puppy*—so they bought it.

Descend to the **main entrance.** After buying your ticket, be sure to pick up the free exhibit audioguide. At the information desk, pick up the small English brochure explaining the architecture and museum layout, and the seasonal *Guggenheim Bilbao* magazine that details the art currently on display.

After presenting your ticket, enter the **atrium.** This acts as the heart of the building, pumping visitors from various rooms on three levels out and back, always returning to this central area before moving on to the next. The architect invites you to caress the sensual curves of the walls. There are virtually no straight lines (except the floor). Notice the sheets of glass that make up the elevator shaft—overlapping each other like a fish's scales. Each glass and limestone panel is unique, designed by a computer and shaped by a robot...as will likely be standard in constructing the great buildings of the future.

From the atrium, step out onto the riverside **terrace.** The "water garden" lets the river symbolically lap at the base of the building. This pool is home to four unusual sculptures (the first two appear occasionally throughout the day): a five-part "fire fountain" (notice the squares in the pool to the right); a "fog sculpture" that billows up from below; another piece by Jeff Koons, *Tulips*, which is a colorful, chrome bouquet of inflated flowers; and the most recent addition, *Tall Tree and the Eye* by British artist Anish Kapoor. Composed of 73 reflective spheres arranged vertically, the sculpture endlessly reflects the Guggenheim, the river, and the beholder.

Still out on the terrace, notice the museum's commitment to public spaces: On the right a grand **staircase** leads under a big green bridge to a tower; the effect wraps the bridge into the museum's grand scheme. The 30-foot-tall **spider,** called *Maman* ("Mommy"), is French artist Louise Bourgeois' depiction of her mother: She spins a beautiful and delicate web of life...which is used to entrap her victims. (It makes a little more sense if you understand that the artist's mother was a weaver. Or maybe not.)

Gehry designed the vast **ground floor** mainly to house often-huge modern-art installations. Computer-controlled lighting adjusts for different exhibits. Surfaces are clean and bare, so you can focus on the art. While most of the collection comes and goes, Richard Serra's huge *Matter of Time* sculpture in the largest gallery (#104) is permanent. Who would want to move those massive metal coils? The intent is to have visitors walk among these metal walls—the "art" is experiencing this journey.

Because this museum is part of the Guggenheim "family" of museums, the **collection** perpetually rotates among the sister Guggenheim galleries in New York and Venice. The best approach to your visit is simply to immerse yourself in a modern-art happening, rather than to count on seeing a particular piece or a specific artist's works.

You can't fully enjoy the museum's architecture without taking a circular stroll up and down each side of the river along the handsome promenade and over the two modern **pedestrian bridges.** (After you tour the museum, you can borrow a free "outdoor audioguide" to learn more—ID required—but it doesn't say much or take you across the river.) The building's skin—shiny and metallic, with a scale-like texture—is made of thin titanium, carefully created to give just the desired color and reflective quality. The external appearance tells you what's inside: The blocky limestone parts contain square-shaped galleries, and the titanium sections hold nonlinear spaces.

As you look out over the rest of the city, think of this: Gehry designed his building to reflect what he saw here in Bilbao. Now other architects are, in turn, creating new buildings that complement his. It's an appealing synergy for this old city.

Leaving the Museum: To get to the Old Town from the Guggenheim, take the tram that leaves from the river level beside the museum, just past the kid-pleasing fountain (ride it in direction: Atxuri). Hop off at the Arriaga stop, near the dripping-Baroque riverfront theater of the same name. From here, cross the street to enter the heart of the Old Town.

NEAR THE GUGGENHEIM
Fine Arts Museum (Museo de Bellas Artes)
Often overshadowed by the Guggenheim, the Fine Arts Museum contains a thoughtfully laid out collection arranged chronologically from the 12th century to the present. Find minor works by many Spanish artists such as Goya, El Greco, Picasso, Murillo, Zurbarán, Sorolla, Chillida, Tàpies, and Barceló—along with a

handful of local painters. Other international artists in the collection include Gauguin, Klee, Bacon, Cassatt, and more. Skip the pedantic €1 audioguide. The museum is at the edge of the lovely Doña Casilda Iturrizar Park, perfect for a stroll after your visit.

Cost and Hours: €7, Wed-Mon 10:00-20:00, closed Tue, last entry 15 minutes before closing, a short walk from the Guggenheim at Museo Plaza 2, Metro stop: Moyúa, tel. 944-396-060, www.museobilbao.com.

Alhóndiga Bilbao

Bilbao's new culture and leisure center, designed by French architect Philippe Starck, is worth a quick visit or a lazy afternoon. Not one of the 43 interior columns is alike—the designs are meant to represent the entirety of materials and styles from antiquity to today. The center houses a cinema, auditorium, exhibition spaces, and restaurant—so it functions as a community gathering space. Most impressive is its glass-bottomed rooftop pool—from the atrium below, visitors can gaze up at backstrokers in the water above.

Cost and Hours: Free entry to the Alhóndiga itself, €10 day pass gives you access to the pool and sundeck; open Mon-Fri 7:00-23:00, Sat 8:30-23:00, Sun 8:30-23:00; 10-minute walk from the Guggenheim at Plaza Arriquibar 4, tel. 944-014-014, www.alhondigabilbao.com.

Funicular de Artxanda

Opened in 1915, this funicular still provides *bilbainos* with a green escape from their somewhat grimy city. The three-minute ride offers sweeping views of the city on the way to the top of Mount Artxanda, where there's a park, restaurants, and a sports complex. Bring a picnic on a sunny afternoon, and take a moment to ponder the giant thumbprint sculpture dedicated to Basque soldiers who fought against Franco during the civil war.

Cost and Hours: €1, leaves every 15 minutes, daily 7:15-22:00, until 23:00 in summer, cross the Zubizuri Bridge and walk two blocks along Calle Mújica y Burton to the cable-car station, Plaza del Funicular, tel. 944-454-966.

OLD TOWN (CASCO VIEJO)

Bilbao's Old Town, with tall, narrow lanes lined with thriving shops and tapas bars, is worth a stroll. Because the weather is wetter here than in many other parts of Spain (hence the green hillsides), the little balconies that climb the outside walls of buildings are glassed in, creating cozy little breakfast nooks.

Whether you want to or not, you'll eventually wind up at Old Bilbao's centerpiece, the **Santiago Cathedral,** a 14th-century Gothic church with a tranquil interior that has been scrubbed clean inside and out (free, €2 to dip into cloister and tiny museum featuring a smiling Jesus—pay the nun; Mon-Fri 10:00-13:00 & 17:00-19:30, closed Sat-Sun; tel. 944-153-627).

Various museums (including those dedicated to diocesan art and the Holy Week processions) are in or near the Old Town, but on a quick visit only one is worth considering...

Basque Museum (Euskal Museoa)

As a leading city of Spain's Basque region, Bilbao has lovingly assembled artifacts of Basque heritage in this 16th-century convent. English pamphlets scattered throughout give wordy yet informative background on the displays.

Cost and Hours: €3, Mon and Wed-Fri 10:00-17:00, Sat 10:00-13:30 & 16:00-19:00, Sun 10:00-14:00, closed Tue, Miguel de Unamuno Plaza 4, tel. 944-155-423, www.euskal-museoa.org/es.

Visiting the Museum: For the most part, follow the museum's standard route—except on the first floor, where it's best to start in Section 3 and end in Section 1.

The main sight in the ground-floor cloister is the Iron-Age *El Mikeldi*, a stone animal figure. The first floor centers on the maritime activities of the seafaring Basques, as well as the pastoral traditional lifestyle of the region's shepherds. The second floor has exhibits covering porcelain, timeworn tools, and ironworks that helped spur the economic prominence of the Basque region.

On the top floor are fragments from two oak trees from Guernica—cherished relics of Basque nationalism.The Arbol Viejo and the Arbol Nuevo each stood for 150 years in front of the Gernika Assembly House until their "clinical death." This floor also has exhibits on the social, political, and economic impact of Bilbao over three centuries.

La Ribera Market

With a new, three-star Michelin restaurant, Bilbao seems poised to give San Sebastián a run for its money as culinary capital of the Basque Country. As part of an urban renewal plan, the 1929 La Ribera city market has recently reopened to an enthusiastic public. Stroll the stalls for the freshest fish (look for the busiest sellers), shop for produce, and admire a series of Art Deco stained-glass panels on the top floor. The city's coat-of-arms, with two wolves, can be found in the largest panels. There's been a market here since Bilbao was founded in 1300.

Cost and Hours: Free entry, Mon and Sat 8:00-15:00, Tue-Fri 8:00-14:30 & 17:00-20:00, closed Sun, tel. 946-023-791, www.mercadodelaribera.net.

Sleeping in Bilbao

(€1 = about $1.40, country code: 34)

Bilbao merits an overnight stay. Even those who are interested only in the Guggenheim find that there's much more to see in this historic yet quickly changing city. All of these accommodations have free Wi-Fi.

NEAR THE GUGGENHEIM MUSEUM

$$$ Gran Hotel Domine Bilbao is *the* place for well-heeled modern-art fans looking for a splurge close to the museum. It's right across the street from the main entrance to the Guggenheim and Jeff Koons' *Puppy.* The hotel is gathered around an atrium with a giant "stone tree" and other artsy flourishes, and its decor (by a prominent Spanish designer) was clearly inspired by Gehry's masterpiece. The 145 plush rooms are distinctly black, white, steel, and very postmodern (standard Db-€130-200, museum-view "executive" rooms for €50 more, rates vary widely with events and demand, breakfast-€26, air-con, elevator, guest computer, great museum-view breakfast terrace, free gym with wet and dry saunas, Alameda Mazarredo 61, tel. 944-253-300, www.granhoteldominebilbao.com, recepcion.domine@hoteles-silken.com). If arriving by tram, take the main museum steps up by the fountains to reach the hotel.

IN THE OLD TOWN

To reach the Old Town, take the tram to the Arriaga stop.

$$ Hotel Bilbao Jardines is a fresh new place buried in the Old Town with 32 modern but basic rooms with squeaky floors (Sb-€58, Db-€75, less off-season, breakfast-€5, quieter rooms in back, air-con, elevator, free rental bicycles, Calle Jardines 9, tel. 944-794-210, www.hotelbilbaojardines.com, info@hotelbilbao jardines.com, Marta, Felix, and Monica).

$$ Tryp Arenal is a chain hotel with simple, business-class rooms and helpful staff in a great location across from the Arriaga Theater (Db-€80, breakfast-€8, air-con, elevator, Calle Los Fueros 2, tel. 944-153-100, www.melia.com, tryp.arenal@melia.com).

$$ Pensión Roquefer, run by petite and friendly Félix and Fabiana, has 12 tidy, charming rooms. Most have a balcony, including some with impressive views of the cathedral (Sb-€50, Db-€65, prices drop in low season, extra bed-€15, Lotería 2, tel. 944-159-755, www.pensionroquefer.com, info@pensionroquefer.com).

$ La Estrella Ostatu is a family-run establishment with 26 simple but neat rooms up a twisty staircase near the Basque Museum. It's on a busy street with several bars—you'll want to bring earplugs (Sb-€35, Db-€60 in summer, cheaper off-season, breakfast-€3-4, María Muñoz 6, tel. 944-164-066, www.la-estrella-ostatu.com,

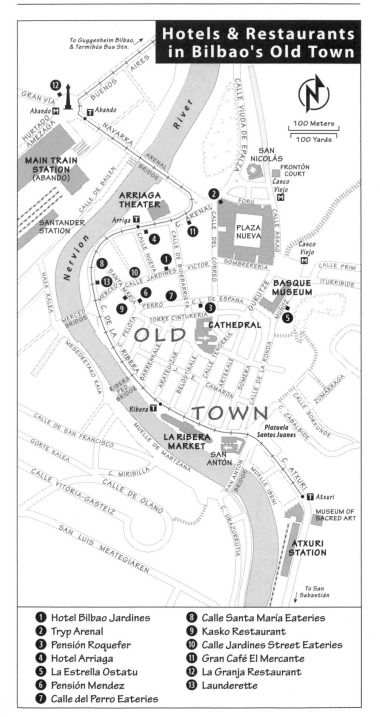

Hotels & Restaurants in Bilbao's Old Town

1. Hotel Bilbao Jardines
2. Tryp Arenal
3. Pensión Roquefer
4. Hotel Arriaga
5. La Estrella Ostatu
6. Pensión Mendez
7. Calle del Perro Eateries
8. Calle Santa María Eateries
9. Kasko Restaurant
10. Calle Jardines Street Eateries
11. Gran Café El Mercante
12. La Granja Restaurant
13. Launderette

laestrellabilbao@yahoo.es, just enough English spoken, Jesus and Begoña).

$ Hotel Arriaga offers 21 traditional but well-maintained rooms and a spirited reception (Sb-€44, Db-€55, extra bed-€16, some rooms overlook a busy street—request a quiet back room, free guest computer, lounge, parking-€8/day, Ribera 3, tel. 944-790-001, www.hotelarriaga.es, info@hotelarriaga.es, Jon). As you cross the bridge from the station, it's just behind the big theater of the same name.

$ Pensión Mendez provides basic accommodations on two different floors, with stoic but professional service. Rooms on the fourth floor share a bathroom (S-€25, Sb-€40, D-€35, Db-€50, T-€50, Tb-€70, extra bed-€15, Calle Santa Maria 13, tel. 944-160-364, www.pensionmendez.com, comercial@pensionmendez.com).

Eating in Bilbao

NEAR THE GUGGENHEIM MUSEUM

The easiest choice is the good **cafeteria** in the museum itself, which features *pintxos*, salads, and sandwiches (upper level, separate entry above museum entry; daily 9:30-20:30 except closed Mon off-season). Adjacent to the cafeteria is the museum's more chic **Bistro.** Try the €18 express lunch or the €25 fixed-price meal offered all day (reservations smart, tel. 944-239-333, http://en.bistroguggenheimbilbao.com).

The circular structure outside the museum by the playgrounds and fountains is a pleasant **outdoor café** serving €2.50 tapas (point at the ones you like on the bar). If the tables are full, you can take your food to one of the stone benches nearby. In the evenings, they sometimes have live music.

The streets in front of the museum have a handful of both sit-down and carry-out eateries (cafés, pizzerias, sandwich shops) to choose from. I like **Zuretzat** for quick and cheap *pintxos*—as do older, salty locals (Iparraguirre 7, tel. 944-248-505). National chain **Fresc Co** is a healthy and cheap option for lunch or dinner, with an all-you-can-eat salad buffet including some hot dishes, dessert, and coffee for about €10 (daily 12:30-24:00, 10-minute walk from the Guggenheim, 3 blocks west of Plaza Moyúa at Gran Vía 55).

IN THE OLD TOWN

Bilbao has developed a thriving restaurant and tapas-bar scene in recent years. You'll find plenty of options on the lanes near the cathedral. Most restaurants around the Old Town advertise a fixed-price lunch for around €12; some close for siesta between 16:00 and 20:00.

Calle del Perro: This street is tops for the tasty little tapas called *pintxos* (PEEN-chohs). **Xukela Bar** is my favorite, with its inviting atmosphere, good wines, and an addictive array of €1.60 tapas spread along its bar (tables only for clients eating hot dishes, Calle del Perro 2, tel. 944-159-772). Calle del Perro is also good for sit-down restaurants. Browse the menus and interiors and choose your favorite. Well-regarded options include three places virtually next door to each other: **Egiluz** (€11 meals served in small restaurant up steep spiral staircase in the back); **Río-Oja** (€8 specialties, focus on shareable traditional dishes called *cazuelitas*); and **Rotterdam** (€10-15 plates, also has *cazuelitas;* try the *chipirones en su tinta*—squids in their own ink, served with a glass of house red for €11).

Calle Santa María: This street caters to a younger crowd, with softer lighting and a livelier atmosphere, and has four bars worth considering: Gatz, Santa María, Kasko, and Con B de Bilbao. **Kasko** is the most upscale option, with stuffy service, a pianist, and an interesting fixed-price dinner (starter, main course, dessert, and good wine served 20:30-23:00 for €27 Sun-Thu and €32 Fri-Sat, Santa Maria 16, tel. 944-160-311, www.restaurante kasko.com). **Con B de Bilbao** serves beautiful and hearty *pintxos* or *montaditos* (*pintxos* decoratively piled high like little mountains) in a trendy, minimalist setting (€2-3 *pintxos*, €6-9 *raciones*, Calle Santa María 9, tel. 944-158-776).

Jardines and Calle del Arenal: Eateries also abound on Jardines street, including the popular Berton and its sister dining room—**Berton Sasibil**—across the lane (meals and *pintxos*, at #11 and #8, closed Mon, tel. 944-167-035). **Gorbea** brings a splash of modernity into the Old Town, with younger but professional wait staff serving generous portions of modern cuisine and traditional Basque classics (at #3, tel. 944-795-482, www.restaurantegorbea.net). **La Deliciosa** is just that—delicious traditional Basque dishes served in a bistro setting (at #1, tel. 944-150-944).

On nearby Calle del Arenal, the **Gran Café El Mercante** is a convivial bar-restaurant that's popular with locals and outgoing tourists. Settle into the Old-World-meets-modernity atmosphere for breakfast, *pintxos*, or just a quick *caña* (beer) any time of day. When it's busy, be assertive to get service. The meek may inherit the earth, but they won't get the waiter's attention here (daily, at #3, tel. 946-084-669).

NEAR THE RENFE TRAIN STATION

There's not much on the main facade to distinguish it, but stepping through **La Granja**'s revolving doors is like entering a time machine. Founded in 1926, the interior seems more like a dusty gentlemen's club than a restaurant. The food at lunchtime is simply presented with proper waiters and classic marble-topped tables. It's a good spot to fuel up on coffee before hopping on the tram to the Guggenheim. The atmosphere becomes less formal and livelier at night (€13.75 fixed-price lunch, daily, at Plaza Circular 3 but look for rear entrance on Calle Ledesma, tel. 944-230-813).

Bilbao Connections

From Bilbao by Bus to: San Sebastián (2/hour, hourly on weekends, 6:30-22:00, 1.25 hours, arrives at San Sebastián's Amara Station), **Guernica** (4/hour, fewer on weekends, 40 minutes), **Lekeitio** (hourly, 1.25 hours), **Pamplona** (5-6/day, 2 hours), **Burgos** (8/day, fewer on weekends, 2-3 hours), **Santander** (hourly, 1.5 hours, transfer there to bus to **Santillana del Mar** or **Comillas**). These buses depart from Bilbao's Termibús Station (www.termibus.es).

By RENFE Train to: Madrid (2-3/day, 5-6.5 hours), **Barcelona** (2/day, 6.5 hours), **Burgos** (2-3/day, 2.5-3 hours), **Salamanca** (3/day, 6 hours), **León** (1/day, 5 hours). Remember, these trains leave from the RENFE station, across the river from the Old Town (tram stop: Abando). A planned new train line (coming in 2017) will connect Bilbao to other cities in a snap (30 minutes to San Sebastián, 2.25 hours to Madrid, 5.5 hours to Paris)—but it's still slow trains for now.

By EuskoTren to: San Sebastián (hourly, long and scenic 2.5-hour trip to San Sebastián's Amara EuskoTren Station), **Guernica** (2/hour, 50 minutes, take Bilbao-Bermeo line, direction: Bermeo). These trains depart from Bilbao's Atxuri Station, just beyond the Old Town past the Ribera Market, tel. 902-543-210, www.euskotren.es.

Pamplona

Proud Pamplona, with stout old walls standing guard in the Pyrenees foothills, is the capital of the province of Navarre ("Navarra" in Spanish). At its peak in the Middle Ages, Navarre was a grand kingdom that controlled parts of today's Spain and France. (The king of Spain, Felipe VI, is a descendant of the French line of Navarre royalty.) After the French and Spanish parts split, Pamplona remained the capital of Spanish Navarre.

Today Pamplona—called "Iruña" in the Basque language—feels at once affluent (with the sleek new infrastructure of a town on the rise), claustrophobic (with its warren of narrow lanes), and fascinating (with its odd traditions, rich history, and ties to Hemingway). Culturally, the city is a lively hodgepodge of Basque and *Navarro*. Locals like to distinguish between *Vascos* (people of Basque citizenship—not them) and *Vascones* (people who identify culturally as Basques—as do many *Navarros*). Pamplona is also an important seat for a controversial wing of the Catholic Church, Opus Dei, founded in Spain in 1928 by the Catholic priest Josemaría Escrivá. He established the private Pamplona-based University of Navarra, and Opus Dei also runs a hospital and several schools in the city.

Of course, Pamplona is best known as the host of one of Spain's (and Europe's) most famous festivals: the Running of the Bulls (held in conjunction with the Fiesta de San Fermín, July 6-14). For latecomers, San Fermín Txikito ("Little San Fermín") offers a less touristy alternative in late September. But there's more to this town than bulls—and, in fact, visiting at other times is preferable to the crowds and 24/7 party atmosphere that seize Pamplona during the festival. Contrary to the chaotic or even backward image that its famous festival might suggest, Pamplona generally feels welcoming, sane, and enjoyable.

Orientation to Pamplona

Pamplona has about 200,000 people. Most everything of interest is in the tight, twisting lanes of the Old Town (Casco Antiguo), centered on the main square, Plaza del Castillo. The newer Ensanche ("Expansion") neighborhood just to the south—with a sensible grid plan—holds several good hotels and the bus station.

TOURIST INFORMATION

Pamplona's well-organized TI is located near the Running of the Bulls Monument. Pick up the handy map/guide and get your questions answered (likely Mon-Sat 10:00-17:00, Sun 10:00-14:00, free

Wi-Fi, Avenida Roncesvalles 4, tel. 848-420-420, www.turismo denavarra.es). The TI sells colorful posters of San Fermín festivities from the 1900s for €0.60. You'll also find a TI next to City Hall (daily 10:00-20:00 in summer, 10:00-14:00 and closed Mon in off-season, closed during Fiesta de San Fermín, on Plaza Consistorial at Calle San Saturnino 2, www.turismodepamplona.es).

ARRIVAL IN PAMPLONA

You can store bags at the bus station, but not at the train station.

By Bus: The sleek, user-friendly bus station is underground along the western edge of the Ensanche area, about a 10-minute walk from the Old Town sightseeing zone. The station has pay Internet terminals and a multilingual information desk that makes trip planning a breeze (Mon-Fri 10:00-14:00 & 15:00-19:00, Sat-Sun 10:00-13:00 & 16:00-19:00). On arrival, go up the escalators, cross the street, turn left, and walk a half-block, where you can turn right down the busy Conde Oliveto street. Along this street, you're near several of my recommended accommodations—or you can walk two blocks to the big traffic circle called Plaza Príncipe de Viana. From here, turn left up Avenida de San Ignacio to reach the Old Town.

By Train: The RENFE station is farther from the center, across the river to the northwest. It's easiest to hop on public bus #9 (€1.50, every 15 minutes), which drops you at the big Plaza Príncipe de Viana traffic circle south of the Old Town (described above)—look for a square with a fountain in the center.

By Car: Everything is well-marked: Simply follow the bull's-eyes to the center of town, where individual hotels are clearly signposted. There's also handy parking right at Plaza del Castillo and Plaza de Toros, where the bullring is (close to several recommended hotels).

By Plane: The Pamplona Airport is located about four miles outside the city (airport code: PNA, tel. 902-404-704, www.aena.es). A taxi from the airport to the city center costs around €12.

HELPFUL HINTS

No Bull—There's Another Fiesta: The last weekend in September, Pamplona celebrates **San Fermín Txikito** ("Little San Fermín"), a bull-free and practically tourist-free festival centered around the church of San Fermín de Aldapa (located behind the Mercado Santo Domingo on Calle Aldapa). Used only for Mass the rest of the year (and housing little of interest except a small statue of the saint), this church opens its doors each fall to become the heart of a celebration involving concerts, brass-band and food competitions, and parades of giant mannequins throughout the city.

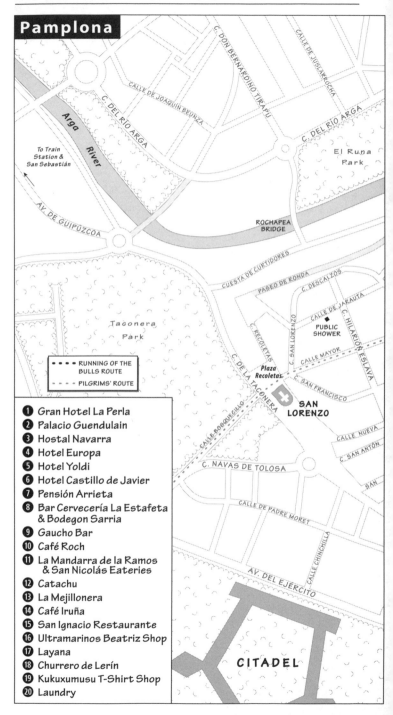

Pamplona

- To Train Station & San Sebastián

--- RUNNING OF THE BULLS ROUTE
--- PILGRIMS' ROUTE

- ❶ Gran Hotel La Perla
- ❷ Palacio Guendulain
- ❸ Hostal Navarra
- ❹ Hotel Europa
- ❺ Hotel Yoldi
- ❻ Hotel Castillo de Javier
- ❼ Pensión Arrieta
- ❽ Bar Cervecería La Estafeta & Bodegon Sarria
- ❾ Gaucho Bar
- ❿ Café Roch
- ⓫ La Mandarra de la Ramos & San Nicolás Eateries
- ⓬ Catachu
- ⓭ La Mejillonera
- ⓮ Café Iruña
- ⓯ San Ignacio Restaurante
- ⓰ Ultramarinos Beatriz Shop
- ⓱ Layana
- ⓲ Churrero de Lerín
- ⓳ Kukuxumusu T-Shirt Shop
- ⓴ Laundry

Map labels: Arga River, C. DEL RIO ARGA, C. DEL RIO ARGA, CALLE DE JOAQUÍN BEUNZA, C. DON BERNARDINO TIRAPU, CALLE DE JUSLARROCHA, El Runa Park, AV. DE GUIPÚZCOA, ROCHAPEA BRIDGE, CUESTA DE CURTIDORES, PASEO DE RONDA, C. DESCALZOS, Taconera Park, C. RECOLETAS, C. SAN LORENZO, CALLE DE JARAUTA, C. HILARIÓN ESLAVA, PUBLIC SHOWER, CALLE MAYOR, Plaza Recoletas, C. DE LA TACONERA, C. SAN FRANCISCO, SAN LORENZO, CALLE BOSQUECILLO, CALLE NUEVA, C. SAN ANTÓN, C. NAVAS DE TOLOSA, SAN, CALLE DE PADRE MORET, CALLE CHINCHILLA, AV. DEL EJÉRCITO, CITADEL

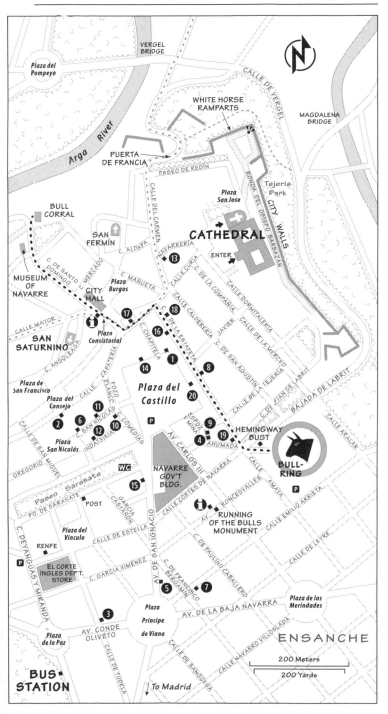

VERGEL BRIDGE

Plaza del Pompeyo

CALLE DE VERGEL

Arga River

WHITE HORSE RAMPARTS

MAGDALENA BRIDGE

PUERTA DE FRANCIA

PASEO DE REDIN

RONDA DEL OBISPO BARBAZAN

Tejeria Park

CITY WALLS

BULL CORRAL

SAN FERMÍN

CALLE DEL CARMEN

Plaza San Jose

CATHEDRAL

ENTER

C. DE SANTO DOMINGO

MUSEUM OF NAVARRE

MERCADO

C. ALDAPA

NAVARRERIA

13

C. CURIA

Plaza Burgos

C. MANUETA

CITY HALL

CALLE ESTAFETA

C. DE LA COMPAÑIA

CALLE DORMITALERIA

CALLE MAYOR

Plaza Consistorial

17

C. CHAPITELA

18

C. DE LA ESTAFETA

C. CALDERERIA

JAVIER

CALLE DE LA MERCED

SAN SATURNINO

CALLE ANSOLEAGA

16

C. DE SAN AGUSTIN

C. DE LA TEJERIA

14

1

8

Plaza de San Francisco

Plaza del Castillo

C. DE JUAN DE LABRIT

BAJADA DE LABRIT

CALLE ZAPATERIA

POZO BLANCO

20

Plaza del Consejo

11

2   **6**

SAN NICOLAS

COMEDIAS

10

ESPOZ Y MINA

9

HEMINGWAY BUST

CALLE ARCALAR

CALLE DE SAN MIGUEL

12

INDATXIKIA

Plaza San Nicolás

AV. CARLOS III

4

19

AHUMADA

BULL-RING

GREGORIO

WC

Paseo   Sarasate

PO. DE SARASATE

GARCIA CASTAÑON

NAVARRE GOV'T BLDG.

15

CALLE CORTES DE NAVARRA

AV.   RONCESVALLES

AMAYA

CALLE EMILIO ARRIETA

POST

AV. SAN IGNACIO

CALLE DE ESTELLA

RUNNING OF THE BULLS MONUMENT

Plaza del Vínculo

RENFE

C. DEVANGUAS Y MIRANDA

EL CORTE INGLES DEP'T. STORE

C. GARCIA XIMENEZ

C. DE FRANCISCO BERGAMIN

C. DE PAULINO CABALLERO

CALLE DE LEYRE

5   **7**

Plaza de las Merindades

3

Plaza Príncipe de Viana

AV. DE LA BAJA NAVARRA

ENSANCHE

AV. CONDE OLIVETO

CALLE DE TUDELA

CALLE DE SANGÜESA

CALLE NAVARRO VILLOSLADA

Plaza de la Paz

BUS STATION

To Madrid

200 Meters

200 Yards

Laundry: EcoLaundry is conveniently located on the main square (washer-€6/load, detergent dispensed automatically, dryer-€2/15 minutes, open daily, last wash at 21:00, Plaza del Castillo 10, tel. 608-333-450).

Local Guide: Francisco Glaría is a top-notch guide and simply a delight to be with (€140/half-day up to 4 hours, mobile 629-661-604, www.novotur.com, francisco@novotur.com).

Pamplona Walk

THE WALKING OF THE TOURISTS

Even if you're not in town for the famous San Fermín festival, you can still get a good flavor of the town by following in the foot- and hoof-steps of its participants. This self-guided walk takes you through the town center along the same route of the famous Running of the Bulls.

• *Begin by the river, at the...*

Bull Corral: During the San Fermín festival, the bulls are released from here at 8:00 each morning (the rest of the year, it's a parked-car corral). They first run up Cuesta de Santo Domingo; signs labeled *El Encierro* mark their route. Follow them.

• *A few blocks ahead on the right is the...*

Museum of Navarre (Museo de Navarra): This museum, worth ▲, has four floors of artifacts and paintings celebrating the art of Navarre, from prehistoric to modern (€2, free Sat afternoons and all day Sun, open Tue-Sat 9:30-14:00 & 17:00-19:00, Sun 11:00-14:00, closed Mon, Santo Domingo 47, tel. 848-426-492, www.cfnavarra.es/cultura/museo). Formerly a 16th-century hospital, the building retains its Neoclassical entrance. Art is displayed chronologically: prehistoric tools and pottery and Roman mosaics on the first floor, Gothic and Renaissance artifacts along with castle frescoes on the second floor, Baroque and 19th- and 20th-century works (including Goya's painting *Retrato de Marques de San Adrian*) on the third floor, and 20th- and 21st-century paintings by local artists on the top floor. The ground floor hosts rotating exhibitions, often of modern art. Spacious and well-arranged, the museum can be toured within an hour—consider circling back here after our walk.

Check out the **adjoining church** (on the left as you exit, show museum ticket), with its impressive golden Baroque-Rococo altarpiece depicting the Annunciation.

• *Continue along Cuesta de Santo Domingo. Embedded in the wall on your right, look for the small shrine containing an image of San Fermín. Farther up on your left is the **food market of Santo Domingo**, a handy spot to buy picnic supplies, including fine local cheeses (supermarket upstairs, market stalls downstairs, Mon-Sat 8:00-14:00, closed Sun).*

Ahead in the square is...

City Hall (Ayuntamiento): When Pamplona was just starting out, many Camino pilgrims who had been "just passing through" decided to stick around.  They helped to build the city you're enjoying today, but tended to cling to their own regional groups, which squabbled periodically. So in 1423, the King of Navarre (Charles III) tore down the internal walls and built a City Hall here to unite the community. This version (late Baroque, from the 18th century) is highly symbolic: Hercules demonstrates the city's strength, while the horn-blower trumpets Pamplona's greatness.

The festival of San Fermín begins and ends on the balcony of this building (with the flags). Look in the direction you just came (also the route of the bulls), and find the line of metal squares in the pavement—used to secure barricades for the run. There are four rows, creating two barriers on each side. The inner space is for press and emergency medical care; spectators line up along the outer barrier. This first stretch is uphill, allowing the bulls to use their strong hind legs to pick up serious momentum.

• *Follow the route of the bulls two blocks down Mercaderes street (next to Alexander Jewelry). Turn right onto...*

La Estafeta Street: At this turn, the bulls—who are now going downhill—begin to lose their balance, often sliding into the barricade. Note that if you want to side-trip to the cathedral—described later, under "Sights in Pamplona"—it's dead ahead, three blocks up the skinny lane called "Curia" from this corner.

Once the bulls regain their footing, they charge up the middle of La Estafeta. Notice how narrow the street is: No room for barricades...no escape for the daredevils trying to outrun the bulls.

On days that the bulls aren't running, La Estafeta is one of the most appealing streets in Pamplona. It's home to some of the best tapas bars in town (see "Eating in Pamplona," later). Because the Old Town was walled right up until 1923, space in here was at a premium—making houses tall and streets narrow.

Partway down the first block on the right, look for the hole-in-the-wall **Ultramarinos Beatriz** shop (at #22)—most locals just call it "Beatriz"—makers of the best treats in Pamplona (Mon-Fri 9:00-14:00 & 16:30-20:00, Sat 9:00-14:00, closed Sun, tel. 948-220-618). Anything with chocolate is good, but the mini-croissants are sensational. They come in three types: *garrotes de chocolate,* filled with milk chocolate; *cabello de angel,* filled with sweet pumpkin fibers;

The Symbols of Santiago

The pilgrim route leading to Santiago de Compostela—and the city itself—are rife with symbolism. Here are a few of the key items you'll see along the way.

- **St. James:** The Camino's namesake is also its single biggest symbol. St. James can be depicted three ways: as a pilgrim, as an apostle, and as a Crusader (slaughtering Moors).

- **The Scallop Shell (Vieira):** Figuratively, the various routes from Europe to Santiago come together like the lines of a scallop shell.  And literally, scallops are abundant on the Galician coast. Though medieval pilgrims carried shells with them only on the return home—to prove they'd been here, and to scoop water from wells— today's pilgrims also carry them on the way to Santiago. The yellow sideways shell that looks like a starburst marks the route for bikers.

- **The Gourd:** Gourds were used by pilgrims to drink water and wine.

- **The Yellow Arrow:** These arrows direct pilgrims at every intersection from France to Santiago.

- **The Red Cross:** This long, skinny cross with curly ends at the top and sides, and ending in a sword blade at the bottom, represents the Knights of Santiago. This 12th-century Christian military order had a dual mission: to battle Muslim invaders while providing hospice and protection to pilgrims along the Camino de Santiago.

- **The Tomb and Star:** St. James' tomb (usually depicted as a simple coffin or box), and the stars that led to its discovery, appear throughout the city of Santiago, either together or separately.

and *manzana,* apple (€3 for a box of six, also sold by weight). So simple...but oh so good.

Halfway down the street, notice the alley on the right leading to the main square (we'll circle back to the square later). Farther down, near the very end of La Estafeta (on the right, at #76), look for the shop called **Kukuxumusu**—Basque for "the kiss of a flea." These whimsical, locally designed cartoon T-shirts are a local favorite. The giant digital clock outside the shop counts down to the next Running of the Bulls.

• *La Estafeta eventually leads you right to Pamplona's...*

Bullring: At the end of the run, the bulls charge down the ramp and through the red door. The bullring is used only nine days each summer (during the festival). The original arena from 1923 was expanded in the 1960s (see the extension at the top), doubling its capacity and halving its architectural charm. Bullfights start at 18:00, and tickets are expensive. But the price plummets if you buy tickets from scalpers after the first or second bull. The audience at most bullfights is silent, but Pamplona's spectators are notorious for their raucous behavior. They're known to intentionally spill things on tourists just to get a reaction...respond with a laugh and a positive attitude, and you'll earn their respect—and you'll probably have the time of your life.

Look for the big bust of **Ernest Hemingway,** celebrated by Pamplona as if he were a native son. Hemingway came here for the first time during the 1923 Running of the Bulls. Inspired by the spectacle and the gore, he later wrote about the event in his classic *The Sun Also Rises.* He said that he enjoyed seeing two wild animals running together: one on two legs, and the other on four. This literary giant put Pamplona and its humble, obscure bullfighting festival on the world map; visitors come from far and wide even today, searching for adventure in Hemingway's Pamplona. He came to his last Running of the Bulls in 1959 and reportedly regretted the attention his writing had brought to what had been a simple local festival. But the people of Pamplona appreciate "Papa" as one of their own. At the beginning of the annual festival, young people tie a red neckerchief around this statue so Hemingway can be properly outfitted for the occasion.

• *Walk 20 yards, keeping the bullring on your left, then cross the busy street and walk a block into the pedestrian zone to the life-size...*

Running of the Bulls Monument (Monumento al Encierro): This statue (from 2007) shows six bulls, two steer, and ten runners in action. Find the self-portrait of the sculptor (bald, lying down, and about to be gored). The statue has quickly become a local favorite, but is not without controversy: There are 10 *mozos* but no *mozas*—where are the female runners?

• *From here you can turn right and walk two blocks up the street to the main square...*

Plaza del Castillo: While not as grand as Spain's top squares, Pamplona's has something particularly cozy and livable about it. It's

dominated by the Navarre government building (sort of like a state capitol). Several Hemingway sights surround this square. The recommended Gran Hotel La Perla, in the corner, was his favorite place to stay. It recently underwent a head-to-toe five-st renovation, but Hemingw

The Running of the Bulls:
Fiesta de San Fermín

"A San Fermín pedimos, por ser nuestro patrón, nos guíe en el encierro, dándonos su bendición."

"We ask San Fermín, because he is our Patron, to guide us through the Running of the Bulls, giving us his blessing."

Song sung before the run

For nine days each July, a million visitors pack into Pamplona to watch a gang of reckless, sangria-fueled adventurers thrust themselves into the path of an oncoming herd of furious bulls. Locals call it *El Encierro* (literally, "the enclosing"—as in, taking the beasts to be enclosed in the bullring)...but everyone else knows it as the "Running of the Bulls."

The festival begins at City Hall at noon on July 6, with various events filling the next nine days and nights. Originally celebrated as the feast of San Fermín—who is still honored by a religious procession through town on July 7—it has since evolved into a full slate of live music, fireworks, general revelry, and an excuse for debauchery. After dark the town erupts into a rollicking party scene. To beat the heat, participants chug refreshing sangria or *kalimotxo* (*calimocho* in Spanish)—half red wine, half cola. The town can't accommodate the crowds, so some visitors day-trip in from elsewhere (such as San Sebastián), and many young tourists simply pass out in city parks overnight (public showers are on Calle Hilarión Eslava in the Old Town).

The Running of the Bulls takes place each morning of the festival and is broadcast nationwide on live TV. The bulls' photos appear in the local paper beforehand, allowing runners to size up their opponents. If you're here to watch, stake your claim at a vantage point along the outer barrier by 6:30 or 7:00 in the morning. Don't try to stand along the inner barrier—reserved  for press and medical personnel—or you'll be evicted when the action begins.

Before the run starts, runners sing a song to San Fermín (see lyrics above) three times to ask for divine guidance. Soon the bulls will be released from their pen near Cuesta de Santo Domingo. From here they'll stampede a half-mile through the town center...with thrill-seekers called *mozos* (and female *mozas*) running in front of the herd, trying to avoid a hoof or horn in the rear end.

Mozos traditionally wear white with strips of red tied around their necks and waists, and carry a newspaper to cover the bull's eyes when they're ready to jump out of the way. Two legends explain the red-and-white uniform: One says it's to honor San Fermín, a saint (white) who was martyred (red); the other says that the runners dress like butchers, who began this tradition. (The bulls are color-blind, so they don't care.)

At 8:00, six bulls are set loose. The beginning of the run is marked by two firecrackers—one for the first bull to leave the pen, and another for the last bull. The animals charge down the street, while the *mozos* try to run in front of them for as long as possible before diving out of the way. The bulls are kept on course by fencing off side-streets (with openings just big enough for *mozos* to escape). Shop windows and doors are boarded up.

A bull becomes most dangerous when separated from the herd. For this reason, a few steer—who are calmer, slower, have bigger horns, and wear a bell—are released with the bulls, and a few more trot behind them to absorb angry stragglers and clear the streets. (There's no greater embarrassment in this *muy macho* culture than to think you've run with a bull...only to realize later that you actually ran with a steer.)

The bulls' destination: the bullring...where they'll be ceremonially slaughtered as the day's entertainment.

If you're considering running with the bulls, it's essential to equip yourself with specific safety information not contained in this book. Locals suggest a few guidelines: First, understand that these are very dangerous animals, and running with them is entirely at your own risk. Be as sober as possible, and wear good shoes to protect your feet from broken glass and from being stepped on by bulls and people. (Runners wearing sandals might be ejected by police.) You're not allowed to carry a backpack, as its motion could distract the bulls. If you fall, wait for the animals to pass before standing up—it's better to be trampled by six bulls than to be gored by one. Ideally, try to get an experienced *mozo* to guide you on your first run.

Cruel as this all seems to the bulls—who scramble for footing on the uneven cobblestones as they rush toward their doom in the bullring—the human participants don't come away unscathed. Each year, dozens of people are gored, trampled, or otherwise injured. Over the last century, 15 runners have been killed at the event. But far more people have died from overconsumption of alcohol.

The festival ends at midnight on July 14, when the townspeople congregate in front of the City Hall, light candles, and sing their sad song, *"Pobre de Mí"*: "Poor me, the Fiesta de San Fermín has ended."

room was kept exactly as he liked it, right down to the furniture he used while writing...and two balconies overlooking the bull action on La Estafeta street. He also was known to frequent Bar Txoko at the top of the square (as well as pretty much every other bar in town) and the venerable Café Iruña at the bottom of the square. The recommended Café Iruña actually has a separate "Hemingway Corner" room, with a life-size statue of "Papa" to pose with.

• *You've survived the run. Now enjoy the rest of Pamplona's sights.*

Sights in Pamplona

▲▲CATHEDRAL (CATEDRAL)

The Camino de Santiago is lined with great cathedrals, making Pamplona's feel like an architectural also-ran. However, after an expensive makeover, it looks like new and holds an interesting museum with a thoughtful message for pilgrims and tourists alike.

Cost and Hours: Cathedral and museum-€5, daily 10:30-19:00, until 17:00 in winter, museum closed Sun and during church services, last entry one hour before closing, tel. 948-212-594.

Visiting the Cathedral: The cathedral—a Gothic core wrapped in a Neoclassical shell—is shiny and clean from the outside, but the interior is dark and mysterious. Follow signs for *entrada* at the left side of the main entrance, buy your ticket, and go inside.

In the back-left corner chapel, dedicated to San Juan Bautista, find the Renaissance **crucifix**—shockingly realistic for a no-name artist of the time (compare it with the more typical one in the next chapel). The accuracy of Christ's musculature leads some to speculate that the artist had a model. (When you drive a nail through a foot, toes splay as you see here...but this is rarely seen on other crucifixes of the time.) It's said that if the dangling lock of hair touches Jesus' chest, the world will end.

The prominent **tomb** dominating the middle of the nave holds Charles III (the king of Navarre who united the disparate groups of Pamplona) and his wife. The blue fleur-de-lis pattern is a reminder that the kings of Navarre once controlled a large swath of France. Notice that Charles' face is realistic, indicating that it was sculpted while he was still alive, whereas his wife's face is idealized—done after she died. Around the base of the tomb, monks from various orders mourn the couple's death.

In the **choir,** look for the statue nicknamed "Mary of the Adopted Child." The Baby Jesus was stolen from this statue in the 16th century and replaced with a different version...which looks nothing like his mother. (The mother, dating from the 13th century, is the only treasure surviving from the previous church that stood on this spot.)

Leave the cathedral and head to the **museum,** in the former cloister and attached buildings. The exhibits document the origins of Western thought and religion without focusing on one particular civilization or geographic area. Pass the spiral staircase into a room that chronicles the stages of cathedral construction. Next, wander through the Gothic cloister to the Archaeology Hall and the main exhibit.

Ramparts View: Exit the cathedral to the left, walking to the tree-lined square. Continue to the small viewpoint overlooking the White Horse Ramparts. This is your best chance to see part of Pamplona's imposing **city walls**—designed to defend against potential invaders from the Pyrenees, still 80 percent intact, and now an inviting parkland. Belly up to the overlook, with views across the city's suburban sprawl. Beyond those hills on the horizon to the left are San Sebastián and the Bay of Biscay. Camino pilgrims enter town through the Puerta de Francia gate below and on the left. This area is popular with people who are in town for the Running of the Bulls but didn't make hotel reservations. Sadly, it's not unusual for people to fall asleep on top of the wall...then roll off to their deaths.

OTHER CHURCHES

As a prominent town on a pilgrim route, Pamplona has its share of other interesting churches. These two are worth a quick visit. They're both on the Camino trail through town; to reach them, simply head west along Calle Mayor from the City Hall Square (near where my self-guided walk begins).

Church of San Saturnino

The most important pilgrim church in Pamplona, this is an architectural combination: a 15th-century Gothic body with an 18th-century Baroque altar. Duck inside: This is where pilgrims can get their credential stamped (someone's usually on duty in the pews). At the end across from where you enter, you'll see an altar with the silver-bodied, golden-haloed Holy Virgin of the Camino. As you continue your journey, you'll notice that most churches along the Camino are dedicated to Mary. According to legend, when St. James himself came on a missionary trip through northern Spain, he suffered a crisis of faith around Zaragoza (not far from here). But, inspired by the Virgin, he managed to complete his journey to Galicia. Pilgrims following in his footsteps find similar inspiration from Mary today.

Cost and Hours: Free, Mon-Sat 9:00-12:30 & 18:00-20:00, Sun 10:15-13:30 & 18:00-20:00.

Church of San Lorenzo

San Fermín is a big name in town, and you'll find him in a giant side-chapel of this church, overlooking the ring road at the edge of the Old Town. Enter the church and turn right down the transept to find the statue of **San Fermín,** dressed in red and wearing a gold miter (tall hat). Pamplona was founded by the Roman Emperor Pompey (hence the name) in the first century B.C. Later, a Roman general here became the first in the empire to allow Christians to worship openly. The general's son—Fermín—even preached the word himself...until he was martyred. Fermín has been the patron saint here ever since. Just below the statue's Adam's apple, squint to see a reliquary holding Fermín's actual finger.

The statue—gussied up in an even more over-the-top miter and staff—is paraded around on Fermín's feast day, July 7, which was the origin of today's bull festival. This chapel is the most popular place in town for weddings.

Cost and Hours: Free, Mon-Sat 8:00-12:30 & 17:30-20:00, Sun 8:30-13:45 & 17:30-20:00.

Sleeping in Pamplona

(€1 = about $1.40, country code: 34)

Because Pamplona is a business-oriented town, prices go up during the week; on weekends (Fri-Sun), you can usually score a discount. When I've listed a range, you can assume the high prices are for weekdays (Mon-Thu). All prices go way, way up for the San Fermín festival, when you must book as far in advance as possible.

$$$ Gran Hotel La Perla is the town's undisputed top splurge. Hemingway's favorite hotel, sitting right on the main square, has recently undergone a top-to-bottom five-star renovation. Its 44 rooms offer luxury at Pamplona's best address (standard Db-€140-270, bigger and fancier rooms-€375-575, rates can drop dramatically—check for deals online, breakfast-€20, air-con, elevator, free guest computer, Wi-Fi, restaurant, Plaza del Castillo 1, tel. 948-223-000, www.granhotellaperla.com, informacion@gran hotellaperla.com). Well-heeled lit lovers can drop €575 for a night in the Hemingway room, still furnished as it was when "Papa" stayed there (with a brand-new bathroom grafted on the front).

$$$ At Palacio Guendulain, pander to your inner aristocrat at a hotel owned by the Count of Guendulain. Currently living in Madrid, he had his mansion in Pamplona converted into a luxurious 25-room hotel decorated with family crests, antiques, Spanish Old Masters, and ultra-modern bathrooms. Check out the collection of carriages in the courtyard (Db *"clasica"*-€110-150, Db *"deluxe"*-€145-185, Db suite-€325-365, extra bed-€54, rates can drop off-season, breakfast-€17, air-con, elevator, guest computer and Wi-Fi, restaurant open to non-guests, Zapateria 53, tel. 948-225-522, www.palacioguendulain.com).

$$ Hostal Navarra is the best value in Pamplona, with 14 modern, well-maintained, clean rooms. Near the bus station, but an easy walk from the Old Town, it's well-run by Miguel, who speaks English (Sb-€45-50, Db-€55-66, 10 percent discount if you mention this book and reserve directly with the hotel through 2015 except in July-Aug, continental breakfast-€7, Wi-Fi, check in from 14:00, reception closes at 22:00—notify if you'll be arriving later, Calle Tudela 9, tel. 948-225-164, www.hostalnavarra.com, info@hostalnavarra.com).

$$ Hotel Europa, a few blocks off the square, offers 21 rooms with reasonable prices for its high class and ideal location (Sb-€69-78, Db-€75-92, continental breakfast-€5, full breakfast-€11, air-con, elevator, Wi-Fi, Calle Espoz y Mina 11, tel. 948-221-800, www.hoteleuropapamplona.com, info@hoteleuropapamplona.com). The ground-floor restaurant is a well-regarded splurge among locals.

$$ Hotel Yoldi is a comfortable business-style hotel in a 19th-century building. Well-located just off Plaza Príncipe de Viana, its 50 modern rooms are handy for travelers arriving by bus from the train station (Sb-€56-66, Db-€72-77, continental breakfast-€5, breakfast buffet-€11, elevator, Wi-Fi, café, Avenida de San Ignacio 11, tel. 948-224-800, www.hotelyoldi.com, yoldi@hotelyoldi.com).

$$ Hotel Castillo de Javier, right on the bustling San Nicolás bar street (request a quieter back room), rents 19 small, simple, yet lovely rooms (Sb-€45, Db-€63, breakfast-€4.40, air-con, elevator, Wi-Fi, Calle San Nicolás 50, tel. 948-203-040, www.hotelcastillo dejavier.com, info@hotelcastillodejavier.com). This is a step up from the several cheap *hostales* that line the same street.

$ Pensión Arrieta is an old-fashioned budget option renting 13 basic rooms in the new part of town. Carmen and Máximo don't speak English, but their daughter Maika does (D-€40, Db-€50, Calle Emilio Arrieta 27, tel. 948-228-459, www.pensionarrieta.net, pensionarrieta@pensionarrieta.net).

Eating in Pamplona

All of these eateries are within a couple minutes' walk of one another, and the tapas bars make a wonderful little pub crawl.

TAPAS CRAWL

On Calle de la Estafeta: The best concentration of trendy tapas bars is on and near the skinny drag called La Estafeta. My favorites here are **Bar Cervecería La Estafeta** (try the *gulas*—baby eels—stuffed in a red pepper, daily, at #54, tel. 948-222-157) and **Bodegon Sarria,** where you'll lick your lips for *escombro,* a hot sandwich with Iberian ham and chorizo (English menu, dining room to enjoy Navarre dishes, at #52, tel. 948-227-713).

Near Plaza del Castillo: **Gaucho Bar** is a proud little prize-winning place serving gourmet tapas cooked to order for €2.50-3 each. You could sit down, enjoy three tapas, and have an excellent meal. I never pass up the *huevo con trufo*—stir the truffle into the egg to get the full effect of the flavors (daily, just a few steps off the main square at Calle Espoz y Mina 7, tel. 948-225-073, ask for English menu).

Café Roch is a time-warp with a line of delightful tapas (€1.60 each). Their most popular are the stuffed pepper and the fried Roquefort (find the tobacco shop at #35 on Plaza del Castillo—it's a block away on the left at Calle de las Comedias 6, tel. 948-222-390).

The narrow and slightly seedy Calle San Nicolás has more than its share of hole-in-the-wall tapas joints, with an older, more traditional clientele, and greasier, more straightforward tapas. **La Mandarra de la Ramos** ("Ramos' Apron"), at #9, is a pork lover's paradise, where cured legs dangle enticingly over your head. Ham it up with a couple of *tostadas de jamón,* best washed down with a glass of the local *vino tinto* (daily, just around the corner from Café Roch, tel. 948-212-654).

Catachu serves ample portions in a simple but eclectic setting (weekly €12 menus, €20 on Fri-Sat, open Sun-Thu 13:00-17:00 & 20:00-24:00—except closed Mon for lunch, Fri-Sat 13:00-24:00, Indatxikia 16, tel. 948-226-028).

Near the Cathedral: **La Mejillonera** satisfies seafood lovers with its simple, homey atmosphere. Order a *caña* (small draft beer) and a *media* (half-portion) *de calamares bravos.* These deep-fried mini-calamari are the perfect vehicle for picking up all that mayo and hot sauce (open Tue-Sun, Calle Navarrería 12, tel. 948-229-184).

RESTAURANTS

Café Iruña, which clings to its venerable past and its connection to Hemingway (who loved the place), serves up drinks out on the main square and food in the delightful old 1888 interior. While the food is mediocre, the ambience is great. Find the little "Hemingway's Corner" (El Rincón de Hemingway) side-eatery in back, where the bearded one is still hanging out at the bar (accessible only

on weekends). Enjoy black-and-white photos of Ernesto, young and old, in Pamplona (€14 fixed-price meal for lunch and dinner, pricier €22 Sat dinner deal, open daily, Plaza del Castillo 44, tel. 948-222-064, www.cafeiruna.com).

San Ignacio Restaurante is an excellent choice for a real restaurant, where Nuntxi serves local fare with an emphasis on seasonal products. Set in what was formerly a private home, this place is elegant and inviting (€5-19 starters, €16-22 main dishes, fixed-price meal-€22 on weekdays or €29 on weekends, open daily for lunch 13:30-15:30, also for dinner Thu-Sat 20:30-22:30, facing the back of the Navarre government building at Avenida San Ignacio 4, tel. 948-221-874, www.restaurantesanignacio.com).

SWEETS

To satisfy a sugar craving, visit the **Ultramarinos Beatriz** shop on Calle de la Estafeta, which sells delicious mini-croissants with various sweet fillings. Or try one of these places:

Layana summons passersby with the thick scent of sugar and butter. A line of locals often spills out the doors because they know that both the *pasta de nata* and the *pasta de mermelada* (cream-filled and marmalade-filled cookies) are worth the wait (Calle Calceteros 12, tel. 948-221-124).

Churrero de Lerín serves the best *churros y chocolate* in Pamplona. The donut-like hoops are perfect with the thick, hot chocolate. Cleanse your palette with a free swig of sweet brandy from the *porrón*, a glass dispenser with a spout like a hummingbird's beak. Be sure to pour from high up and avoid touching your mouth to the spout. You're welcome to add graffiti to the walls...as long as you don't write about politics or religion (€2.50/half-dozen *churros*, €2 chocolate, Calle de la Estafeta 5).

Pamplona Connections

Note that the bus station is closer to the Old Town than the train station, and that most connections are faster by bus anyway.

From Pamplona by Bus to: Burgos (3/day with change in Vitoria, 3-4 hours), **San Sebastián** (8-10/day, 1 hour), **Bilbao** (5-6/day, 2 hours), **Madrid** (7/day, 5 hours), **Madrid Barajas Airport** (6/day, 5-6 hours; this bus may serve other airports in the future—see www.alsa.es; buy ticket online or from the driver). For bus schedules, see www.autobusesdenavarra.com, tel. 948-203-566.

By Train to: Burgos (2-3/day, 2-3.5 hours, better option than bus—fast train leaves at midday), **San Sebastián** (2/day, 1.75 hours), **León** (2/day, 4-5.5 hours), **Madrid** (4/day direct, 3 hours).

French Basque Country (Le Pays Basque)

Compared to their Spanish cousins across the border, the French Basques seem French first and Basque second. You'll see less Euskara writing here than in Spain, but these destinations have their own special spice, mingling Basque and French influences with beautiful rolling countryside and gorgeous beaches.

Just 45 minutes apart by car, San Sebastián and St-Jean-de-Luz bridge the Spanish and French Basque regions. Between them you'll find the functional towns of Irún (Spain) and Hendaye (France), and the delightful hill town of Hondarribia, which is worth a visit if you have time to spare.

My favorite home base here is the central, comfy, and manageable resort village of St-Jean-de-Luz. It's a stone's throw to Bayonne (with its "big-city" bustle and good Basque museum) and the snazzy beach town of Biarritz. A drive inland rewards you with a panoply of adorable French Basque villages. And St-Jean-de-Luz is a relaxing place to "come home" to, with its mellow ambience, fine strolling atmosphere, and good restaurants.

St-Jean-de-Luz / Donibane Lohizune

St-Jean-de-Luz (san zhahn-duh-looz) sits cradled between its small port and gentle bay. The days when whaling, cod fishing, and pirating made it wealthy are long gone, but don't expect a cute Basque backwater. Tourism has become the economic mainstay, and it shows. Pastry shops serve Basque specialties, and store windows proudly display berets (a Basque symbol). Ice-cream lickers stroll traffic-free streets, while soft, sandy beaches tempt travelers to toss their itineraries into the bay. The knobby little mountain La Rhune towers above the festive scene. Locals joke that if it's clear enough to see La Rhune's peak, it's going to rain, but if you can't see it, it's raining already.

The town has little of sightseeing importance, but it's a good base for exploring the Basque Country and a convenient beach and port town that provides the most enjoyable dose of Basque culture in France. The town fills with French tourists in July and August—especially the first two weeks of August, when it's practically impossible to find a room without a reservation made long in advance...or even walk down the main street.

It Happened at Hendaye

If taking the train between the Spanish and French Basque regions, you'll change trains at the nondescript little Hendaye Station. While it seems innocent enough, this was the site of a fateful meeting between two of Europe's most notorious 20th-century dictators.

In the days before World War II, Adolf Hitler and Francisco Franco maintained a diplomatic relationship. But after the fall of France, they decided to meet secretly in Hendaye, to size each other up. On October 23, 1940, Hitler traveled through Nazi-occupied France, then waited impatiently on the platform for Franco's delayed train. The over-eager Franco hoped the Führer would invite him to join in a military alliance with Germany (and ultimately share in the expected war spoils).

According to reports of the meeting, Franco was greedy, boastful, and misguided, leading Hitler to dismiss him as a buffoon. Franco later spun the situation by claiming that he had cleverly avoided being pulled into World War II. In fact, his own incompetence is what saved Spain. Had Franco made a better impression on Hitler here at Hendaye, it's possible that Spain would have entered the war, which could have changed the course of Spanish, German, and European history.

Orientation to St-Jean-de-Luz

St-Jean-de-Luz's old city lies between the train tracks, the Nivelle River, and the Atlantic. The main traffic-free street, Rue Gambetta, channels walkers through the center, halfway between the train tracks and the ocean. The small town of Ciboure, across the river, holds nothing of interest.

The only sight worth entering in St-Jean-de-Luz is the church where Louis XIV and Marie-Thérèse tied the royal knot (Eglise St. Jean-Baptiste, described later). St-Jean-de-Luz is best appreciated along its pedestrian streets, lively squares, and golden, sandy beaches. With nice views and walking trails, the park at the far eastern end of the beachfront promenade at Pointe Ste. Barbe makes a good walking destination.

TOURIST INFORMATION

The helpful TI is next to the big market hall, along the busy Boulevard Victor Hugo (July-Aug Mon-Sat 9:00-19:30, Sun 10:00-13:00 & 15:00-19:00; Sept-June Mon-Sat 9:00-12:30 & 14:00-19:00, Sun 10:00-13:00—except Jan-March, when it's closed Sun; 20 Boulevard Victor Hugo, tel. 05 59 26 03 16, town info: www.saint-jean-de-luz.com, regional info: www.terreetcotebasques.com).

Dipping into France

If you're heading from Spain to France, you don't have to worry about currency changes—both countries use the euro—or lengthy border stops (although police might ask to see your passport on trains going into Spain). Here are a few other practicalities:

Phones: France's telephone country code is 33. Spanish phone cards and stamps will not work in France. If you have a mobile phone with a Spanish SIM card, it should work here—but at a higher rate per minute (although texting is cheap).

Hours: France typically does not enjoy the same "siesta" as Spain, so shops don't close for a mid-afternoon break. The French eat lunch and dinner closer to the European mainstream time (around 12:00-13:30 & 19:00-21:00)—much earlier than Spaniards do.

Hotel Tips: The French have a simple hotel-rating system based on amenities, indicated in this chapter by asterisks. One star is modest, two has most of the comforts, and three is generally a two-star place with a fancier lobby and more elaborately designed rooms. Four or five stars offer more luxury than you'll probably have time to appreciate.

Restaurant Tips: In France, if you ask for the *menu* (muh-noo), you won't get a list of dishes; you'll get a fixed-price meal. *Menus*, which include three or four courses, are generally a good value if you're hungry: You'll get your choice of soup, appetizer, or salad; your choice from three or four main-course options with vegetables; plus a cheese course and/or a choice of desserts. Service is included (*service compris* or *prix net*), but wine and other drinks generally are extra.

ARRIVAL IN ST-JEAN-DE-LUZ

By Train or Bus: From the train station, the pedestrian underpass leads to the bus station. From there, it's easy to get to the TI and the center of Old Town (just a few blocks away—see map).

By Car: Follow signs for *Centre-Ville,* then *Gare* and *Office de Tourisme.* The Old Town is not car-friendly, with one-way lanes that cut back and forth across pedestrian streets. It's best to park your car in the free parking lot next to the train station.

By Plane: The nearest airport is Biarritz-Anglet-Bayonne Airport, 10 miles to the northeast near Biarritz. The tiny airport is easy to navigate, with a useful TI desk (airport code: BIQ, airport tel. 05 59 43 83 83, www.biarritz.aeroport.fr). To reach St-Jean-de-Luz, you can take a public bus (€3, 7/day, 45 minutes, get off at the Halte Routière stop near the train station, tel. 05 59 26 06 99, www.transports-atcrb.com) or a 25-minute taxi ride (about €30).

French Survival Phrases: Although some French Basques speak Euskara, most speak French in everyday life. You'll find these phrases useful:

Good day.	*Bonjour.*	bohn-zhoor
Mrs./Ma'am	*Madame*	mah-dahm
Mr./Sir	*Monsieur*	muhs-yuh
Please?	*S'il vous plaît?*	see voo play
Thank you.	*Merci.*	mehr-see
You're welcome.	*De rien.*	duh reo-an
Excuse me.	*Pardon.*	par-dohn
Yes./No.	*Oui./Non.*	wee/nohn
Okay.	*D'accord.*	dah-kor
Cheers!	*Santé!*	sahn-tay
Goodbye.	*Au revoir.*	oh ruh-vwahr
women/men	*dames/hommes*	dahm/ohm
one/two/three	*un/deux/trois*	uhn/duh/trwah
Do you speak English?	*Parlez-vous anglais?*	par-lay voo ahn-glay

HELPFUL HINTS

Market Days: The Les Halles covered market is open daily from 7:30 to 13:00 and offers everything from fresh fish and produce to regional specialty dried goods. On Tuesday and Friday mornings (and summer Saturdays) until about 13:00, there's also a street market. Farmers' stands spill through the streets from the market on Boulevard Victor Hugo, giving everyone a rustic whiff of "life is good."

Supermarkets: There are two **Petit Casino** groceries. One is across from the market hall next to the TI, and a smaller one is at the east end of Rue Gambetta near Boulevard Thiers (closed Sun). The bigger and hipper **Carrefour City** is at the intersection of Rue Gambetta and Boulevard Victor Hugo, near the recommended Hôtel Le Petit Trianon (Mon-Sat 7:00-21:00, Sun 9:00-13:00).

Internet Access: The **TI** has free Wi-Fi. **Boutik D Clics** has a handful of computers with Internet access (€1/10 minutes, €5.50/hour; also offers photocopying services; Mon-Fri 9:15-

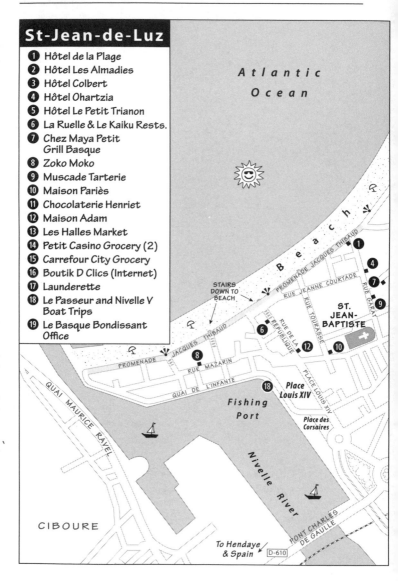

St-Jean-de-Luz

1. Hôtel de la Plage
2. Hôtel Les Almadies
3. Hôtel Colbert
4. Hôtel Ohartzia
5. Hôtel Le Petit Trianon
6. La Ruelle & Le Kaiku Rests.
7. Chez Maya Petit Grill Basque
8. Zoko Moko
9. Muscade Tarterie
10. Maison Pariès
11. Chocolaterie Henriet
12. Maison Adam
13. Les Halles Market
14. Petit Casino Grocery (2)
15. Carrefour City Grocery
16. Boutik D Clics (Internet)
17. Launderette
18. Le Passeur and Nivelle V Boat Trips
19. Le Basque Bondissant Office

12:45 & 14:15-19:00, Sat 9:00-12:00, closed Sun, shorter hours off-season; 5 Rue Chauvin Dragon, tel. 05 59 51 24 48).

Pharmacies: Several can be found on Rue Gambetta. Look for the green cross.

Laundry: Laverie Automatique du Port is at 4 Boulevard Thiers (self-service wash—€5.20/load, dryer—€1/8 minutes, daily 7:00-21:00, change machine; full-service available Tue-Fri 9:30-12:30 & 14:30-18:00; mobile 06 80 06 48 36).

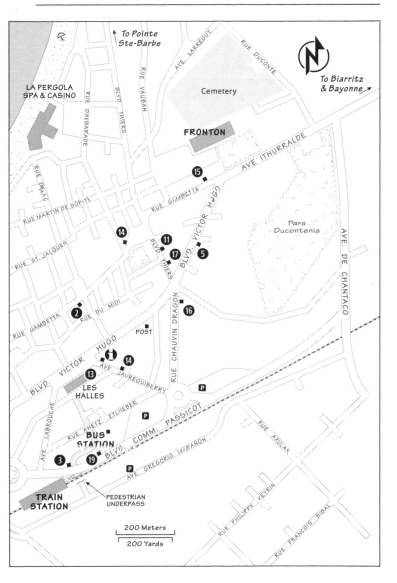

Car Rental: Avis, at the train station, is handiest (Mon-Fri 8:00-18:00, Sat 9:00-18:00, closed Sun, tel. 05 59 26 79 66).

Tours in St-Jean-de-Luz

Tourist Train
A little tourist train does a 30-minute trip around town (€6, departs every 45 minutes from the port, runs April-Oct 10:30-

Pelota

In keeping with their seafaring, shipbuilding, and metalworking heritage, Basque sports are often feats of strength: Who can lift the heaviest stone? Who can row the fastest and farthest?

But the most important Basque sport of all is *pelota*—similar to what you might know as jai alai. Players in white pants and red scarves or shirts use a long, hook-shaped wicker basket (called a *txistera* in Euskara) to whip a ball (smaller and far bouncier than a baseball) back and forth off walls at more than 150 miles per hour. This men's-only game can be played with a wall at one or both ends of the court. Most matches are not professional, but betting on them is common. It can also be played without a racket—this handball version is used as a starter game for kids. Children use a bouncy rubber ball, while adults use a ball with a wooden center that's rather rough on the hands and needs a lot of strength to keep moving.

It seems that every small Basque town has two things: a church and a *pelota* court (called *frontón*). While some *frontóns* are simple and in poor repair, others are freshly painted as a gleaming sign of local pride.

The TI in St-Jean-de-Luz sells tickets and has a schedule of matches throughout the area; you're more likely to find a match in summer (almost daily at 21:00 July-mid-Sept, afternoon matches sometimes on Sat-Sun). Matches are held throughout the year (except for winter) in the villages (ask for details at TI). The professional *cesta punta* matches on Tuesdays and Fridays often come with Basque folkloric half-time shows.

19:00, no train Nov-March, mobile 06 85 70 72 85). It's only worth the money if you need to rest your feet.

Bus Excursions
Le Basque Bondissant runs popular day-trip excursions, including a handy jaunt to the Guggenheim Bilbao (€35 round-trip, includes €13 museum admission, Wed only, departs 9:30 from green bus terminal across the street from train station, returns 19:30). Other itineraries include Ainhoa, Espelette, St-Jean-Pied-de-Port, Loyola and the Cantabrian coast, San Sebastián, and a trip to the *ventas* (discount stores in the foothills of the Pyrenees). You can get information and buy tickets at the TI, or visit the Le Basque Bondissant office in the bus station (Mon-Fri 8:45-12:00 &

13:30-17:30 except closed Wed afternoon, closed Sat-Sun, tel. 05 59 26 30 74, www.basque-bondissant.com). Advance reservations are recommended in winter, when trips are canceled if not enough people sign up.

Boat Trips
Le Passeur, at the port, offers bay crossings to Socoa and Ciboure. Departures come every 40 minutes (€2.50 each way, €18/10 trips—sharable among groups, runs May-mid-Sept, no guides; Quai Maréchal Leclerc, mobile 06 11 69 56 93). **Nivelle V** offers mini-Atlantic cruises and excursions, including half-day fishing trips (€35) departing at 8:00. They offer two coastal excursions: a Basque Coast to Spain tour (€17, 2 hours, leaves at 14:00) and a Sea Cliff tour (€10, 45 minutes, leaves at 16:00). Get tickets at their portside kiosk (runs April-mid-Oct, reservations required July-Aug, Quai Maréchal Leclerc, mobile 06 09 73 61 81, www.croisiere-saintjeandeluz.com).

St-Jean-de-Luz Walk

To get a feel for the town, take this hour-long self-guided stroll. You'll start at the port and make your way to the historic church.

Port: Begin at the little working port (at Place des Corsaires, just beyond the parking lot). Pleasure craft are in the next port over, in Ciboure. Whereas fishing boats used to catch lots of whales and anchovies, now they take in sardines and tuna—and take out tourists on joyrides. Anchovies, once a big part of the fishing business, were overfished nearly into extinction, so they've been protected by the EU for the last few years (though now some limited fishing is permitted).

St-Jean-de-Luz feels cute and nonthreatening now, but in the 17th century it was home to the Basque Corsairs. With the French government's blessing, these pirates who worked the sea—and enriched the town—moored here.

• *After you walk the length of the port, on your right is the tree-lined...*

Place Louis XIV: The town's main square, named for the king who was married here, is a hub of action that serves as the town's communal living room. During the summer, the bandstand features traditional Basque folk music and dancing at 21:00 (almost nightly July-Aug, otherwise Sun and Wed). Facing the square is the City Hall (Herriko Etchea) and the **House of Louis XIV** (he lived here for 40 festive days in 1660). A visit to this house is worthwhile only if you like period furniture, though it's only open for part of the year; the rest of the time the privately owned mansion is occupied by the same family that's had it for over three centuries (€5, June-mid-Oct Wed-Mon, closed Tue and mid-Oct-

July, visits by 40-minute guided tour only, 2-4/day, in French with English handouts, tel. 05 59 26 27 58, www.maison-louis-xiv.fr).

The king's visit is memorialized by a small black equestrian statue at the entrance of the City Hall (a miniature of the huge statue that marks the center of the Versailles courtyard). The plane trees, with truncated branches looking like fists, are cut back in the winter so that in the summer they'll come back with thick, shady foliage.

• *Opposite the port on the far side of the square is...*

Rue de la République: This historic lane leads from Place Louis XIV to the beach. Once the home of fishermen, today it's lined with mostly edible temptations. Facing the square, **Maison Adam** (at #4) still uses the family recipe to bake the macaroons Louis XIV enjoyed during his visit to wed Princess Marie-Thérèse in 1660. Get one for €1.50 or grab other sweets, such as the less historic but just as tasty *gâteau basque*—a baked tart with a cream or cherry filling. Their gourmet shop next door (at #6) has Basque delicacies, *tartelettes*, sandwiches, and wine—great for an epicurean picnic.

Don't eat your fill of dessert just yet, though, because farther down Rue de la République you'll find **Pierre Oteiza,** stacked with rustic Basque cheeses and meats from mountain villages (with a few samples generally out for the tasting, and handy €3.50 paper cones of salami or cheese slices—perfect for munching during this walk; closed 13:00-14:00).

You'll likely eat on this lane tonight. The recommended **Le Kaiku,** the town's top restaurant, fills the oldest building in St-Jean-de-Luz (with its characteristic stone lookout tower), dating from the 1500s. This was the only building on the street to survive a vicious 1558 Spanish attack. Each end of the street is flanked by a cannon, which may be from Basque pirate ships. At the upper end of the street, notice the photo of fisherwomen with baskets on their heads, who would literally run to Bayonne to sell their fresh fish.

• *Continue to the...*

Beach: A high embankment protects the town from storm waters, but generally the Grande Plage—which is lovingly groomed daily—is the peaceful haunt of sun-seekers, soccer players, and happy children. Walk the elevated promenade (to the right). Various tableaux tell history in French. Storms (including a particularly disastrous one in 1749) routinely knocked down buildings. Repeated flooding around 1800 drove the population down by two-thirds. Finally, in 1854, Napoleon III—who had visited here and appreciated the town—began building the three breakwaters you see today. Decades were spent piling 8,000 fifty-ton blocks, and by 1895 the town was protected. To develop their tourist trade, they built a casino and a fine hotel, and even organized a special getaway train from Paris. During those days there were as many visitors as residents (3,000).

• *Stroll through the seaside shopping mall fronting the late–Art-Deco-style La Pergola, which houses a casino and the Hélianthal spa center (entrance around back) and overlooks the beach. Anyone in a white robe strolling the beach is from the spa. Beyond La Pergola is the pink, Neo-Romantic Grand Hôtel (c. 1900), with an inviting terrace for an expensive coffee break (€7 cappuccino). From here circle back into town along Boulevard Thiers until you reach the bustling...*

Rue Gambetta: Turn right at the tiny square called Parc Jean Moulin (kitty-corner from the pharmacy) and circle back to your starting point, following the town's lively pedestrian shopping street. You'll notice many stores selling the renowned *linge Basque*—cotton linens such as tablecloths, napkins, and dishcloths, in the characteristic Basque red, white, and green. There are as many candy shops as there are tourists. Keep an eye open for a local branch of the British auction house Christie's, which specializes in high-end real estate. Video screens in the window advertise French castles for a mere €2 million, while local vacation homes go for considerably less.

• *Just before Place Louis XIV, you'll see the town's main church.*

Eglise St. Jean-Baptiste: The marriage of Louis XIV and Marie-Thérèse put St-Jean-de-Luz on the map, and this church is where it all took place. The ultimate in political marriages, the knot tied between Louis XIV and Marie-Thérèse in 1660 also cinched a reconciliation deal between Europe's two most powerful countries. The king of Spain, Philip IV—who lived in El Escorial palace—gave his daughter in marriage to the king of France, who lived in Versailles. This marriage united Europe's two largest palaces, which helped end a hundred years of hostility and forged an alliance that enabled both to focus attention on other matters (like England). Little St-Jean-de-Luz was selected for its 15 minutes of fame because it was roughly halfway between Madrid and Paris, and virtually on the France-Spain border. The wedding cleared out both Versailles and El Escorial palaces, as anyone who was anyone attended this glamorous event.

The church, centered on the pedestrian street Rue Gambetta, seems modest enough from the exterior...but step inside (Mon-Sat 8:00-12:00 & 14:00-18:30, Sun 8:00-12:00 & 15:00-19:30). The local expertise was in shipbuilding, so the ceiling resembles the hull of a ship turned upside down. The

dark wood balconies running along the nave segregated the men from the women and children (men went upstairs until the 1960s, as they still do in nearby villages) and were typical of Basque churches. The number of levels depended on the importance of the church, and this church, with three levels, is the largest Basque church in France.

The three-foot-long paddle-wheel ship hanging in the center was a gift from Napoleon III's wife, Eugènie. It's a model of an ill-fated ship that had almost sunk just offshore when she was on it. The box seats across from the pulpit were reserved for leading citizens who were expected to be seen in church and set a good example. Today the mayor and city council members sit here on festival Sundays.

The 1670 Baroque altar feels Franco-Spanish and features 20 French saints, with the city's patron saint—St. John the Baptist—placed prominently in the center. Locals in this proud and rich town call it the finest altar in the Basque Country. To see it better, pay €1 to switch on the automatic light (next to the scene of the crucifixion in the nave). The place has great acoustics, and the 17th-century organ is still used for concerts (around €10, mostly in summer, get schedule at TI or online at www.orgueluz.c.la, tickets available at door and possibly in advance at the TI).

As you leave the church, turn left to find the bricked-up door-way—the church's original entrance. According to a quaint but untrue legend, it was sealed after the royal marriage (shown on the wall to the right in a photo of a painting) to symbolize a permanent closing of the door on troubles between France and Spain.

Sleeping in St-Jean-de-Luz

(€1 = about $1.40, country code: 33, * = French hotel rating system, 0-5 stars)

Hotels are expensive here. The higher prices are for peak season (generally July-Sept). In winter, some prices drop below those I've listed. At all of my listings, Wi-Fi is free but breakfast is not included. Those wanting to eat and sleep for less will do slightly better just over the border, in San Sebastián.

$$$ Hôtel de la Plage* has the best location, right on the ocean. Its 22 rooms, 16 with ocean views, have a lively yellow-and-blue modern nautical decor. The contemporary seaview breakfast room doubles as a comfortable lounge (Db-€89-119, view Db-€119-169, family rooms for up to 5-€30 per extra person, breakfast-€11 but free for kids, air-con, elevator, parking-€15/day, 33 Rue Garat, tel. 05 59 51 03 44, www.hoteldelaplage.com, reservation@ hoteldelaplage.com, run by friendly Pierre, Laurent, and Frederic).

$$$ Hôtel Les Almadies,* on the main pedestrian street,

is a bright boutique hotel with seven flawless rooms, comfy public spaces with clever modern touches, a pleasant breakfast room and lounge, an inviting sun deck, and a caring owner (Db-€100-135, higher prices are for rooms with tubs, buffet breakfast-€12, parking-€10/day, 58 Rue Gambetta, tel. 05 59 85 34 48, www.hotel-les-almadies.com, hotel.lesalmadies@wanadoo.fr, Monsieur and Madame Hargous will charm you with their Franglish).

$$$ Hôtel Colbert,*** a Best Western, has 34 modern, tastefully appointed rooms across the street from the train station (Sb-€80-133, Db-€96-162, extra bed-€15, family room-€241-339, breakfast-€14, air-con, elevator, private parking-€20/day or park for free at lot next to train station, 3 Boulevard du Commandant Passicot, tel. 05 59 26 31 99, www.hotelcolbertsaintjeandeluz.com, contact@hotelcolbertsaintjeandeluz.com).

$$ Hôtel Ohartzia** ("Souvenir"), one block off the beach, is comfortable, clean, and peaceful, with the most charming facade I've seen. It comes with 17 simple but well-cared-for rooms, generous and homey public spaces, and a delightful garden. Several rooms are 21st-century modern with vivid colors, and two have small, interior terraces. Higher prices are for the four rooms with tubs (mid-July-Sept Db-€88-99, March-mid-July Db-€78-82, less off-season, extra bed-€15, breakfast-€8, 28 Rue Garat, tel. 05 59 26 00 06, www.hotel-ohartzia.com, hotel.ohartzia@wanadoo.fr). Their front desk is technically open only 8:00-21:00, but owners Madame and Monsieur Audibert (who speak little English) live in the building; their son Benoît speaks English well.

$$ Hôtel Le Petit Trianon,** on a major street a couple of blocks above the Old Town's charm, is simple, bright, and *très sympa* (very nice), with 25 tidy rooms and an accommodating staff (July-Sept Db-€95, Tb-€115, Qb-€160; off-season Db-€75, Tb-€105, Qb-€125; closed mid-Nov-mid-Feb, air-con in most rooms, breakfast-€8.50, limited parking-€10/day, 56 Boulevard Victor Hugo, tel. 05 59 26 11 90, www.hotel-lepetittrianon.com, lepetittrianon@wanadoo.fr). To get a room over the quieter courtyard, ask for *côté cour* (koh-tay koor).

Eating in St-Jean-de-Luz

St-Jean-de-Luz restaurants are known for offering good-value, high-quality cuisine. You can find a wide variety of eateries in the old center. For forgettable food with unforgettable views, choose from several places overlooking the beach. Most places serve from 12:15 to 14:00, and from 19:15 on. Remember, in France *menu* means a fixed-price, multicourse meal.

The traffic-free Rue de la République, which runs from Place Louis XIV to the ocean promenade, is lined with hardworking restaurants (two of which are recommended below). Places are empty at 19:30, but packed at 20:30. Making a reservation, especially on weekends or in summer, is wise. Consider a fun night of bar-hopping for dinner in San Sebastián instead (an hour away in Spain).

La Ruelle serves good, traditionally Basque cuisine—mostly seafood—in a convivial dining room packed with tables, happy eaters, and kitschy Basque decor. André and his playful staff obviously enjoy their work, which gives this popular spot a relaxed and fun ambience. They offer a free sangria to diners with this book. Portions are huge; their €20 *ttoro* (seafood stew) easily feeds two—splitting is OK if you order two starters (€20-25 *menus,* closed Tue-Wed Oct-May, 19 Rue de la République, tel. 05 59 26 37 80).

Le Kaiku is *the* gastronomic experience in St-Jean-de-Luz. They serve modern, creatively presented cuisine, and specialize in wild seafood (rather than farmed). This dressy place is the most romantic in town, but manages not to be stuffy (€27 weekday lunch *menus,* €19 starters, €26-36 main courses, closed Tue-Wed except July-Aug, 17 Rue de la République, tel. 05 59 26 13 20, www.kaiku. fr, Serge and Julie). For the best experience, talk with Serge about what you like best and your price limits (about €60 will get you a three-course meal *à la carte* without wine).

Chez Maya Petit Grill Basque serves hearty traditional Basque cuisine. Their €18 *ttoro* was a highlight of my day. They have €22 and €32 *menus,* but à la carte is more interesting. If you stick around in warm weather, you'll see the clever overhead fan system kick into action (closed for lunch Mon and Thu and all day Wed, 2 Rue St. Jacques, tel. 05 59 26 80 76).

Zoko Moko offers Mediterranean nouvelle cuisine, with artistic creations on big plates. Get an *amuse-bouche* (an appetizer chosen by the chef) and a *mignardise* (a fun bite-sized dessert) with each main plate ordered. The lunchtime *menu du marché* changes weekly, depending on what's fresh in the market (€20 express lunch, €26 lunchtime *menu du marché,* €43 *menu* served all day; open Mon-Sat 12:30-14:00 & 19:30-22:00 except closed Mon July-Sept, closed Sun year-round; Rue Mazarin 6, tel. 05 59 08 01 23, www.zoko-moko.com, owner Charles).

Fast and Cheap: Peruse the takeaway crêpe stands on Rue Gambetta. For a sit-down salad or a sizeable and shareable tart—either sweet or savory—consider **Muscade Tarterie** (€8-13 per slice; closed Mon; 20 Rue Garat, tel. 05 59 26 96 73).

Sweets: **Maison Pariès** is a favorite for its traditional sweets. Locals like their fine chocolates, *tartes,* macaroons, fudge (*kanougas),* and *touron* (like marzipan, but firmer), which comes in a multitude of flavors—brought by Jews who stopped here just over the border in 1492 after being expelled from Spain. The delectable chocolate version of the *gâteau basque* is also worth a try (9 Rue Gambetta, tel. 05 59 26 01 46).

Chocolaterie Henriet has been a regional favorite since 1946. Walk into this quaintly elegant, confectionary world, and take your pick. Chocolates are priced per gram. My favorite is the *Rochers de Biarritz*—chocolate-covered roasted almonds with just a hint of orange (10 Boulevard Thiers—just off of Rue Gambetta, tel. 05 59 22 08 42).

St-Jean-de-Luz Connections

The train station in St-Jean-de-Luz is called St-Jean-de-Luz-Ciboure. Its handy departure board displays lights next to any trains leaving that day. Buses leave from the green building across the street; use the pedestrian underpass to get there. There is reduced bus and rail service on Sundays and off-season.

From St-Jean-de-Luz by Train to: Bayonne (hourly, 25 minutes), **St-Jean-Pied-de-Port** (5/day, 6/day in summer, 2 hours with transfer in Bayonne), **Paris** (5/day direct via high-speed TGV, 5.5 hours; more with transfer in Bordeaux, 6 hours), **Bordeaux** (7/day, 2.5 hours), **Sarlat** (1/day, 2/day on weekends, 6-8 hours, transfer in Bordeaux), **Carcassonne** (1/day, 5 hours, transfers likely in Bayonne and Toulouse).

By Train to San Sebastián: First, take the 10-minute train to the French border town of Hendaye (Gare SNCF stop, about 10/day). Or get to Hendaye by bus (about hourly, 35 minutes, described next); check the schedule to see which leaves first.

Leave the Hendaye SNCF train station to the right, and look for the small building on the same side of the street, where you'll catch the commuter EuskoTren into San Sebastián (usually 4/hour Mon-Fri, 2/hour Sat-Sun, runs 7:00-22:33, 35 minutes). Locals call this line the Topo ("Mole"), since part of it runs underground.

By Bus: ATCRB buses leave from the bus station directly across from the train station. All tickets are bought on the bus. Local ATCRB bus #816 connects St-Jean-de-Luz to **Biarritz** and **Bayonne** almost hourly. It also goes the opposite direction to **Hendaye** about hourly. Be sure to check times and final destinations on the well-displayed timetable at the bus stop post (fewer departures on weekends). Bus #24 connects St-Jean-de-Luz to **Sare** (Mon-Fri 6/day, Sat 2/day, none Sun, 30 minutes, tel. 09 70 80 90 74, www.transports-atcrb.com). A Spanish Pesa bus runs to **San Sebastián**—catch it on the street, in front of the green kiosk next to the bus station (Mon-Sat only, 2/day direct—likely at 12:45 and 19:15, none on Sun, 1 hour, only 1/week off-season, info in Spain tel. 902-101-210, www.pesa.net).

By Excursion: If you're without a car, consider using **Le**

Basque Bondissant's day-trip excursions to visit otherwise difficult-to-reach destinations, such as the Guggenheim Bilbao (see "Tours in St-Jean-de-Luz," earlier).

By Taxi to San Sebastián: This will cost you about €75 for up to four people, but it's convenient (tel. 05 59 26 10 11 or mobile 06 25 76 97 69).

ROUTE TIPS FOR DRIVERS

A one-day side-trip to both Bayonne and Biarritz is easy from St-Jean-de-Luz. These three towns form a sort of triangle (depending on traffic, each one is less than a 30-minute drive from the other). Hop on the autoroute to Bayonne, sightsee there, then take D-810 into Biarritz. Leaving Biarritz, continue along the coastal D-810. In Bidart, watch (on the right) for the town's proud *frontón* (*pelota* court) and stop for a photo of the quaint town hall. Consider peeling off to go into the village center of Guéthary, with another *frontón* and a massive town hall. If you're up for a walk on the beach, cross the little bridge in Guéthary, park by the train station, and hike down to the walkway along the surfing beach (lined with cafés and eateries). When you're ready to move on, you're a very short drive from St-Jean-de-Luz.

Bayonne / Baiona

To feel the urban pulse of French Basque Country, visit Bayonne—modestly but honestly nicknamed "your anchor in the Basque Country" by its tourist board.
With frequent, fast train and bus connections with St-Jean-de-Luz, Bayonne makes an easy half-day side-trip.

Come here to browse through Bayonne's atmospheric and well-worn-yet-lively Old Town, and to admire its impressive Museum

of Basque Culture. Known for establishing Europe's first whaling industry and for inventing the bayonet, Bayonne is more famous today for its ham *(jambon de Bayonne)* and chocolate.

Get lost in Bayonne's Old Town. In pretty Grand Bayonne, tall, slender buildings, decorated in Basque fashion with green-and-red shutters, climb above cobbled streets. Be sure to stroll the streets around the cathedral and along the banks of the smaller Nive River, where you'll find the market (Les Halles).

Orientation to Bayonne

Bayonne's two rivers, the grand Adour and the petite Nive, divide the city into three parts: St-Esprit, with the train station; and the more interesting Grand Bayonne and Petit Bayonne, which together make up the Old Town.

TOURIST INFORMATION

The TI is in a modern parking lot a block off the mighty Adour River, on the northeastern edge of Grand Bayonne. They have very little in English other than a map and a town brochure (July-Aug Mon-Sat 9:00-19:00, Sun 10:00-13:00, March-June and Sept-Oct Mon-Fri 9:00-18:30, Sat 10:00-18:00, closed Sun; shorter hours in off-season; Place des Basques, tel. 08 20 42 64 64, www.bayonne-tourisme.com). There's a pay WC in the back.

ARRIVAL IN BAYONNE

By Train: The TI and Grand Bayonne are a 15-minute walk from the train station: Walk straight out of the station, cross the parking lot and traffic circle, and then cross the imposing bridge (Pont St. Esprit). Once past the big Adour River, continue across a smaller bridge (Pont Mayou), which spans the smaller Nive River. Stop on Pont Mayou to orient yourself: You just left Petit Bayonne (left side of Nive River); ahead of you is Grand Bayonne (spires of cathedral straight ahead, TI a few blocks to the right). The Museum of Basque Culture is in Petit Bayonne, facing the next bridge up the Nive River.

By Car or Bus: The handiest parking is also where buses arrive in Bayonne: next to the TI at the modern parking lot on the edge of Grand Bayonne. To reach the town center from here, walk past the war memorial and through the break in the ramparts. Follow the walkway until you reach a fancy gate that leads through a tunnel. After the tunnel, turn right at the next street; the cathedral should immediately come into view. Continue behind the cathedral and walk down, down, down any of the atmospheric streets to find Les Halles (the market) and the Nive River.

To reach this parking lot, **drivers** take the *Bayonne Sud* exit from the autoroute, then follow green *Bayonne Centre* signs, then white *Centre-Ville* signs (with an *i* for tourist information). You'll see the lot on your right. Payment machines only accept coins for a maximum of two hours. In high season, when this lot can be full, use one of the lots just outside the center (follow signs to *Glain* or *Porte d'Espagne* as you arrive in town), then catch the little orange *navette* (shuttle bus) to get into the center (free, find route maps posted at stops in town, every 7 minutes, Mon-Sat 7:30-19:30, closed Sun).

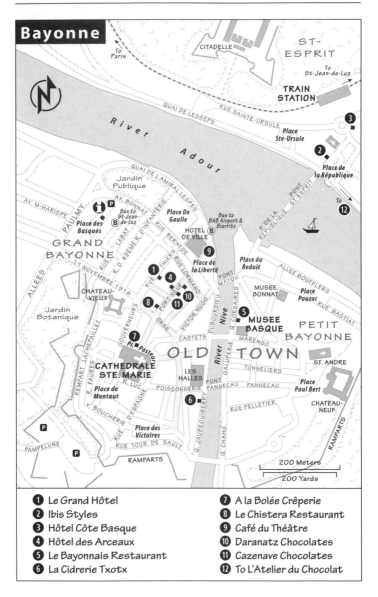

Bayonne

1 Le Grand Hôtel
2 Ibis Styles
3 Hôtel Côte Basque
4 Hôtel des Arceaux
5 Le Bayonnais Restaurant
6 La Cidrerie Txotx
7 A la Bolée Crêperie
8 Le Chistera Restaurant
9 Café du Théâtre
10 Daranatz Chocolates
11 Cazenave Chocolates
12 To L'Atelier du Chocolat

HELPFUL HINTS

Loaner Bikes: Although Bayonne's sights are easily reached on foot (except the chocolate workshop), pedaling about by bike is simple and relaxing. The TI lends a limited number of orange bikes for free to adults during office hours (must leave passport or driver's license and a €150 deposit, same hours and contact information as TI, www.cyclocom.fr).

Laundry: Laverie d'Espagne is just blocks from the cathedral (self-service €4/wash, daily 8:00-20:00, 6 Rue d'Espagne, tel. 05 59 59 54 03).

Sights in Bayonne

▲Museum of Basque Culture (Musée Basque)

This museum (in Petit Bayonne, facing the Nive River at Pont Marengo) explains French Basque culture from cradle to grave—in French, Euskara, and Spanish. The only English you'll read is "do not touch" (unless you buy their informative €5 English booklet). Artifacts and videos take you into traditional Basque villages and sit you in the front row of time-honored festivals, letting you envision this otherwise hard-to-experience culture.

Cost and Hours: €6.50, free first Sun of month, July-Aug daily 10:00-18:30, Thu until 20:30; off-season generally Tue-Sun 10:30-18:00, closed Mon; last entry one hour before closing, 37 Quai des Corsaires, tel. 05 59 59 08 98, www.musee-basque.com.

Visiting the Museum: On the ground floor, you'll begin with a display of carts and tools used in rural life, then continue past some 16th-century gravestones. Look for the *laiak*—distinctive forked hoes used to work the ground. At the end of this section you'll watch a grainy film on Basque rural lifestyles.

The next floor up begins by explaining that the house *(etxea)* is the building block of Basque society. More than just a building, it's a social institution—Basques are named for their house, not vice versa. You'll see models and paintings of Basque houses, then domestic items, a giant door, kitchen equipment, and furniture (including a combination bench table, next to the fireplace). After an exhibit on Basque clothing, you'll move into the nautical life, with models, paintings, and actual boats. The little door leads to a large model of the port of Bayonne in 1805, back when it was a strategic walled city.

Upstairs you'll learn that the religious life of the Basques was strongly influenced by the Camino de Santiago pilgrim trail, which passes through their territory. One somber room explains Basque funeral traditions. The section on social life includes a video of Basque dances (typically accompanied by flute and drums). These are improvised, but according to a clearly outlined structure—not unlike a square dance.

The prominence given to the sport of *pelota* indicates its importance to these people. One dimly lit room shows off several types of *txistera* baskets (*chistera* in French), gloves, and balls used for the game; videos show you how these items are made. The museum wraps up with a brief lesson on the region's history from the 16th to the 20th centuries, including exhibits on the large

Jewish population here (who had fled from a hostile Spain) and the renaissance of Basque culture in the 19th century.

Cathédrale Ste. Marie

Bankrolled by the whaling community, this cathedral sits dead-center in Grand Bayonne and is worth a peek. Find the unique keystones on the ceiling along the nave, then circle behind the church to find the peaceful and polished 13th-century cloisters.

Cost and Hours: Cathedral—free, Mon-Sat 8:00-12:30 & 15:00-17:00, Sun 8:00-12:00 & 15:30-18:00; cloisters—free, daily 9:00-12:30 & 14:00-17:00, until 18:00 mid-May-mid-Sept.

Sweets Shops

With no more whales to catch, Bayonne turned to producing mouthwatering chocolates and marzipan; look for shops on the arcaded Rue du Port Neuf (running between the cathedral and the Adour River). **Daranatz** is Bayonne's best chocolate shop, with bars of chocolate blended with all kinds of flavors—one with a general mix of spices (lots of cardamom), one with just cinnamon, and another with *piments d'Espelette* (15 Arceaux Port Neuf, tel. 05 59 59 03 55, www.chocolat-bayonne-daranatz.fr). **Cazenave,** founded in 1854, is a fancy *chocolaterie* with a small café in the back. Try their foamy hot chocolate with fresh whipped cream on the side, served with buttered toast for €9 (Tue-Sat 9:00-12:00 & 14:00-19:00, closed Sun-Mon, 19 Rue Port Neuf, tel. 05 59 59 03 16, www.chocolats-cazenave.fr).

Chocolate Workshop

L'Atelier du Chocolat is a chocolate factory and boutique in an industrial part of town. You'll see a detailed exhibit on the history and making of chocolate, some workers making luscious goodies (9:30-11:00 only), and a video. The generous chocolate tasting at the end is worth the ticket price for chocoholics.

Cost and Hours: €5.80, Mon-Sat 9:30-12:30 & 14:00-18:00, closed Sun, last entry 1.5 hours before closing, 7 Allée de Gibéléou, tel. 05 59 55 70 23, www.atelierduchocolat.fr.

Getting There: Take city bus #A2 from the TI or the Mairie stop across from the town hall (buy €1 ticket on board), get off at the Jean-Jaurès stop, walk under the railway bridge past the round-about, and follow signs.

Ramparts

The ramparts around Grand Bayonne are open for walking and great for picnicking (access from park at far end of TI parking lot). However, the ramparts do not allow access to either of Bayonne's castles—both are closed to the public.

Sleeping in Bayonne

(€1 = about $1.40, country code: 33, * = French hotel rating system, 0-5 stars)

All of the following listings have free Wi-Fi.

$$$ **Le Grand Hôtel*** is the best of the limited options in Bayonne—it's well-located in Grand Bayonne, with all the comforts and a pleasant staff. While renovating their old building, the owners took care to maintain the original, classic decor (Sb-€75-160, Db-€81-166, breakfast-€15, elevator, parking-€13/day, 21 Rue Thiers, tel. 05 59 59 62 00, www.legrandhotelbayonne.com, info@legrandhotelbayonne.com.

$$$ **Ibis Styles Bayonne Gare Centre*** sits next to the Pont Saint Esprit near the train station. Some of its 45 white, bright rooms overlook the river (Sb-€88-120, Db-€96-135, Tb-€100-145, includes breakfast, elevator, parking-€8/day, 1 Place de la République, tel. 05 59 55 08 08, www.ibis.com, h8716@accor.com).

$$ **Hôtel Côte Basque** is conveniently located by the train station in the Saint Esprit neighborhood, just across the river from the Old Town. It's on a busy street, but the small-but-comfortable rooms have double-paned windows to cut the noise (Sb-€61-66, Db-€65-70, Tb-€71-76, breakfast-€10, elevator, 2 Rue Maubec, tel. 05 59 55 10 21, www.hotel-cotebasque.fr, hotelcotebasque@orange.fr).

$$ **Hôtel des Arceaux** is a family-run B&B-style establishment with 16 rooms on a small pedestrian street in Grand Bayonne. It's just around the corner from the cathedral (Db-€66-76, breakfast-€7, 26 Rue Port Neuf, tel. 05 59 59 15 53, www.hotel-arceaux.com, hotel.arceaux@wanadoo.fr).

Eating in Bayonne

The Grand Bayonne riverside has several tapas restaurants, a couple of easy *bistrots*, and a pizza place. The Petit Bayonne riverside has some *bistrots* and a few more proper sit-down restaurants. The pedestrian streets surrounding the cathedral in Grand Bayonne offer casual dining spots serving crêpes, *tartines*, quiches, and salads. Most places have outdoor tables in nice weather.

Le Bayonnais, next door to the Museum of Basque Culture, serves traditional Basque specialties à la carte. Sit in the blue-tiled interior or out along the river (€20 weekday lunch and dinner *menu*, closed Sun-Mon, 38 Quai des Corsaires, tel. 05 59 25 61 19).

La Cidrerie Txotx (pronounced "choch") has a Spanish-bodega ambience under a chorus line of hams. You can also sit outside, along the river, just past the market hall (€8-12 Basque tapas or €12-19 *plats*, €26 *menu*, daily, 49 Quai Amiral Jauréguiberry, tel. 05 59 59 16 80).

A la Bolée serves up inexpensive sweet and savory crêpes in a cozy atmosphere along the side of the cathedral (daily, 10 Place Pasteur, tel. 05 59 59 18 75).

Le Chistera, run by a family that's spent time in the US, proudly serves traditional Basque dishes made with market-fresh ingredients. Try the *poulet* with Basque sauce or one of their soups, and polish off your meal with homemade *gâteau basque* (€16 lunch *menu*, €25-30 dinners, Tue-Wed 12:00-14:00, Thu-Sun 12:00-14:00 & 19:30-21:00, closed Mon, 42 Rue Port Neuf, tel. 05 59 59 25 93, www.lechistera.com).

Café du Théâtre has pleasant outdoor tables by the river. Try it for a simple early breakfast (8 Place de la Liberté, tel. 05 59 59 09 31).

Picnic Supplies: If the weather's good, consider gathering a picnic from the shops along the pedestrian streets, at Les Halles market (only open in the mornings), in the Casino minimart (Mon-Sat 8:00-13:00 & 15:30-20:00, closed Sun, 38 Rue Port Neuf), or at the Monoprix (Mon-Sat 8:30-20:30, closed Sun, 8 Rue Orbe). Don't forget the chocolate, then head for the park around the ramparts below the *Jardin Botanique* (benches galore).

Bayonne Connections

Chronoplus buses run throughout the area regularly. Most lines run two to three times an hour from about 7:00 to 20:00, but are noticeably less frequent on Saturdays and even sparser on Sundays. Buy a €1 ticket on the bus; if you plan to ride twice or more in one day, buy the 24-hour ticket for €2 (tel. 05 59 52 59 52, www.chronoplus.eu).

From Bayonne by Bus to: BAB (Biarritz-Anglet-Bayonne) Airport (2-3/hour, 15 minutes, line #C is best option), **Biarritz** (2-3/hour, fewer on Sun, 30 minutes, Chronoplus lines #A1 and #A2), and **St-Jean-de-Luz** (almost hourly, 45 minutes, ATCRB line #816). Pick up BAB and Biarritz buses by the Mairie/Théâter stop on the riverside; catch the St-Jean-de-Luz bus from Place des Basques by the TI. Buses to the inland Basque villages of Espelette and Ainhoa are impractical.

By Train to: St-Jean-Pied-de-Port (3-5/day, 1.25 hours).

By Taxi to: **Biarritz** (20 minutes, about €30) and **St-Jean-de-Luz** (30 minutes, about €50—or more if traffic is heavy, tel. 05 59 59 48 48).

Biarritz / Biarritz

A glitzy resort town steeped in the belle époque, Biarritz (bee-ah-ritz) is where the French Basques put on the ritz. In the 19th

century, this simple whaling harbor became, almost overnight, a high-class aristocrat-magnet dubbed the "beach of kings." Although St Jean de Luz and Bayonne are more fully French and more fully Basque, the made-for-international-tourists, jet-set scene of Biarritz is not without its charms. Perched over a popular surfing beach, anchored by grand hotels and casinos, hemmed in by jagged and picturesque rocky islets at either end, and watched over by a lighthouse on a distant promontory, Biarritz is a striking beach resort. However, for sightseers with limited time, it's likely more trouble than it's worth.

Orientation to Biarritz

Biarritz feels much bigger than its population of 30,000. The town sprawls, but virtually everything we're interested in lines up along the waterfront: the beach, the promenade, the hotel and shopping zone, and the TI.

TOURIST INFORMATION

The TI is in a little pink castle two blocks up from the beach (just above the beach and casino, hiding behind the City Hall—look for *hôtel de ville* signs). Pick up the free map and get details on any sightseeing that interests you (July-Aug daily 9:00-19:00; Sept-June Mon-Fri 9:00-18:00, Sat-Sun 10:00-17:00, shorter weekend hours in winter; Square d'Ixelles, tel. 05 59 22 37 00, www.biarritz.fr).

ARRIVAL IN BIARRITZ

By Car: Drivers follow signs for *Centre-Ville*, then carefully track signs for specific parking garages. The most central garages are called *Grande Plage, Casino, Bellevue,* and *St. Eugénie* (closest to the water). Signs in front of each tell you whether it's full *(complet)*, in which case move on to the next one.

By Bus: Buses stop at "Biarritz Centre," a parking lot next to the TI (buses to/from Bayonne stop along the side of the lot; buses to/from St-Jean-de-Luz stop at the end of the lot). If you're taking a bus, be aware that some stop at the outskirts of town—only take one to "Centre."

Don't bother taking the **train** to or from Biarritz, as the station is about two miles from the tourist area (but if you must, Chronoplus bus #A1 connects the train station to the city center hourly, €1, buy ticket from driver).

There is no baggage storage in Biarritz.

Sights in Biarritz

There's little of sightseeing value in Biarritz. The TI can fill you in on the town's four museums (Marine Museum—described later; Chocolate Planet and Museum—intriguing, but a long walk from the center; Oriental Art Museum—large, diverse collection of art from across Asia; and Biarritz Historical Museum—really?).

Your time is best spent strolling along the various levels that climb up from the sea. (Resist the urge to check out the pebble beach for now.) From the TI, you can do a loop: First head west on the lively **pedestrian streets** that occupy the plateau above the water, which are lined with restaurants, cafés, and high-class, resorty window-shopping. (Place Georges Clemenceau is the grassy "main square" of this area.) Biarritz is picnic-friendly, with *beaucoup* benches facing the waves. Consider stocking up before continuing this walk.

Work your way past the Église Sainte Eugénie out to the point with the **Marine Museum** (Musée de la Mer). The most convenient of Biarritz's attractions, this pricey Art Deco museum/aquarium wins the "best rainy-day option" award, with a tank of seals and a chance to get face-to-teeth with live sharks (€13.50, generally daily 9:30-20:00, July-Aug until 24:00, Nov-March until 19:00, closed most of Jan, last entry one hour before closing, tel. 05 59 22 75 40, www.musee delamer.com).

Whether or not you're visiting the museum, it's worth hiking down to the entrance, then wandering out on the walkways that connect the big offshore rocks. These lead to the so-called **Virgin Rock** (Rocher de la Vierge), topped by a statue of Mary. Spot any surfers?

From here stick along the water as you head back toward the

TI. After a bit of up and down over the rocks, don't miss the trail down to **Fishermen's Wharf** (Port des Pêcheurs), a little pocket of salty authenticity that clings like barnacles to the cliff below the hotels. The remnants of an aborted construction project from the town's glory days, this little fishing settlement of humble houses and rugged jetties seems to faintly echo the Basque culture that thrived here before the glitz hit. Many of the houses have been taken over by the tourist trade (gift shops and restaurants).

Continuing along the water (and briefly back up to street level), make your way back to the town's centerpiece, the **big beach** (Grande Plage). Dominating this inviting stretch of sand is the Art Deco casino, and the TI is just above that. If you haven't yet taken the time on your vacation to splash, wade, or stroll on the beach...now's your chance.

Biarritz Connections

From Biarritz by Bus to: St-Jean-de-Luz (nearly hourly, fewer on Sundays, 45 minutes, ATCRB line #816, tel. 09 70 80 90 74, www. transports-atcrb.com) and **Bayonne** (2-3/hour, fewer on Sundays, 30 minutes, Chronoplus lines #A1 and #A2, tel. 05 59 52 59 52, www.chronoplus.eu).

Villages in the French Basque Country

Traditional villages among the green hills, with buildings colored like the Basque flag, offer the best glimpse of Basque culture. Cheese, hard cider, and *pelota* players are the primary products of these villages, which attract few foreigners but many French summer visitors. Most of these villages have welcomed pilgrims bound for Santiago de Compostela since the Middle Ages. Today's hikers trek between local villages or head into the Pyrenees. The most appealing villages lie in the foothills of the Pyrenees, spared from beach-scene development.

Use St-Jean-de-Luz as your base to visit the Basque sights described below. For information on another French Basque village a bit farther away—St-Jean-Pied-de-Port (Donibane Garazi), the starting point of the Camino de Santiago pilgrim trail. You can reach some of these places by public transportation, but the hassle outweighs the rewards.

Do a circuit of these towns in the order they're listed here (and, with time, also add St-Jean-Pied-de-Port at the end). Assuming you're driving, I've included route instructions as well.
• *Only 15 minutes from St-Jean-de-Luz, follow signs for Ascain, then Sare. On the twisty-turny road toward Sare, you'll pass the station for the train up to...*

LA RHUNE/LARRUN

Between the villages of Ascain and Sare, near the border with Spain, a small cogwheel train takes tourists to the top of La Rhune, the region's highest peak (2,969 feet). You'll putt-putt up the hillside for 35 minutes in a wooden, open-air train car to reach panoramic views of land and sea (adults-€15 round-trip, kids-€8, all pay €2-3 more in summer, runs March-mid-Nov daily, closed mid-Nov-Feb, departures weather-dependent—the trip is worthless if it's not clear, goes every 35 minutes when busiest July-Aug, tel. 05 59 54 20 26, www.rhune.com). For those traveling without a car, **Le Basque Bondissant** runs a shuttle for peak-season tourists from St-Jean-de-Luz (€17, kids-€10, train ticket included).

• *Continue along the same road, and look out for pull-offs with room for a couple of cars, typically placed at the most scenic spots. Stop to smell the grass before the next stop...*

SARE/SARA

Sare, which sits at the base of the towering mountain La Rhune, is among the most picturesque villages—and the most touristed. It's easily reached from St-Jean-de-Luz by bus or car. The small TI is on the main square and offers free Wi-Fi (Mon-Fri 9:30-12:30 & 14:00-18:00, Sat 9:30-12:30, closed Sun year-round and Sat Nov-March, tel. 05 59 54 20 14, www.sare.fr). Nearby is a cluster of hotels and the town church (which has an impressive interior, with arches over the gold-slathered altar and Basque-style balconies lining the nave). Reforms in the 18th century prohibited burials at or near Catholic churches, but Basque-style tombstones still surround the main church. At the far end of the square is the town's humble *frontón* (*pelota* court).

• *Leaving Sare, first follow signs for* toutes directions, *then* St-Pée, *and watch for the turnoff to...*

AINHOA/AINHOA

Ainhoa is a colorful, tidy, picturesque one-street town that sees fewer tourists (which is a good thing). Its chunks of old walls and gates mingle with red-and-white half-timbered buildings. The 14th-century church—  with a beautiful golden *retable* (screen behind the altar)—and the *frontón* share center stage. Parking is plentiful; resist the urge to turn off at the *frontón*— it's better to continue on for parking near the TI.

Ainhoa is also a popular starting point for hikes into the hills.

For a spectacular village-and-valleys view, drive five minutes (or walk 90 sweaty minutes) up the steep dirt road to the Chapelle de Notre-Dame d'Aranazau ("d'Aubepine" in French). Start in the central parking lot directly across the main street from the church, then head straight uphill into the clouds. Follow signs for *oratoire*, then count the giant white crosses leading the way to the top. The chapel is occasionally closed, and cloudy days don't offer spectacular views, but the ethereal experience is worth the steep detour for drivers.

• As you leave Ainhoa, you'll have to backtrack the way you came in to find the road to...

ESPELETTE/EZPELETA

Espelette won't let you forget that it's the capital of the region's AOC red peppers *(piments d'Espelette)*, with strands of them dangling like good-luck charms from many houses and storefronts. After strolling the charming, cobbled center, head to the well-restored château and medieval tower of former local barons, which now houses the town hall, exhibition space, and the **TI** (Mon-Fri 9:00-12:30 & 14:00-18:00, Sat 9:30-12:30, shorter hours off-season, closed Sun year-round, tel. 05 59 93 95 02, www.espelette.fr). Or wander downhill toward the pink *frontón*, following the *église* signs past houses constructed in the 1700s and a  captivating stream, to find the town church. Climb up into the church balconies for some fancy views.

Sleeping and Eating: For a good regional meal, consider the **$$ Hôtel Euzkadi**** restaurant, with a *muy* Spanish ambience (€18-35 *menus*, daily 12:30-14:00 & 19:30-21:00, July-Aug closed Mon, Sept-June closed Mon-Tue, 285 Karrika Nagusia, tel. 05 59 93 91 88). The hotel has 27 rooms with modern touches and a swimming pool (Db-€80-85, air-con, elevator, free Wi-Fi, www.hotel-restaurant-euzkadi.com).

• From Espelette, if you have time, you can follow signs to Cambo les Bains, *then* St-Jean-Pied-de-Port *(40 minutes).*

PRACTICALITIES

This section covers just the basics on traveling in Spain and France (for much more information, see *Rick Steves Spain*). You can find free advice on specific topics at www.ricksteves.com/tips.

Money

Spain and France use the euro currency: 1 euro (€) = about $1.40. To convert prices in euros to dollars, add about 40 percent: €20 = about $28, €50 = about $70. (Check www.oanda.com for the latest exchange rates.)

The standard way for travelers to get euros is to withdraw money from ATMs (which locals call a *cajero automático* in Spain and a *distributeur* in France) using a debit or credit card, ideally with a Visa or MasterCard logo. Before departing, call your bank or credit-card company: Confirm that your card(s) will work overseas, ask about international transaction fees, and alert them that you'll be making withdrawals in Europe. Also ask for the PIN number for your credit card in case it'll help you use Europe's "chip-and-PIN" payment machines (see below); allow time for your bank to mail your PIN to you. Memorizing your credit card's PIN lets you use it at some chip-and-PIN machines—just enter your PIN when prompted. To keep your valuables safe, wear a money belt.

Dealing with "Chip and PIN": Much of Europe—including Spain and France—is shifting to a "chip-and-PIN" security system for credit and debit cards, and some merchants rely on it exclusively. (European chip-and-PIN cards are embedded with an electronic security chip, and require the purchaser to punch in a PIN rather than sign a receipt.) If you happen to encounter chip and PIN, it will probably be at payment machines, such as those at train stations, toll roads, or self-serve gas pumps. On the outside chance that a machine won't take your card, don't panic. Find a cashier who can make your card work (they can print a receipt for you to sign), or find a machine that takes cash. You can always use an ATM to withdraw cash with your magnetic-stripe card, even in countries where people predominantly use chip-and-PIN cards.

Phoning

Smart travelers use the telephone to reserve or reconfirm rooms, reserve restaurants, get directions, research transportation connections, confirm tour times, phone home, and lots more.

To call from the US or Canada: For Spain, dial 011-34 and then the local number. (The 011 is our international access code, and 34 is Spain's country code.) For France, dial 011-33 and then the local number, omitting the initial zero. (France's country code is 33.)

To call from a European country to Spain or France: If calling Spain, dial 00-34 followed by the local number. (The 00 is Europe's international access code.) When calling France, dial 00-33 followed by the local number, omitting the initial zero.

To call within Spain or France: Just dial the local number.

To call from either Spain or France to another country: Dial 00 followed by the country code (for example, 1 for the US or Canada), then the area code and number. If calling European countries whose phone numbers begin with 0, you'll usually have to omit that 0 when you dial.

Tips on Phoning: A mobile phone—whether an American one that works in Spain and France, or a European one you buy when you arrive—is handy, but can be pricey. If traveling with a smartphone, switch off data-roaming until you have free Wi-Fi. With Wi-Fi, you can use your smartphone to make free or inexpensive domestic and international calls by taking advantage of a calling app such as Skype, FaceTime, or Google+ Hangouts.

To make cheap international calls while in Spain and France from any phone (even your hotel-room phone), you can buy an international phone card (called a *tarjeta telefónica con código* in Spain, and a *carte à code* in France). These work with a scratch-to-reveal PIN code at any phone, allows you to call home to the US for pennies a minute, and also works for domestic calls within Spain or within France.

Another option is buying an insertable phone card (called a *tarjeta telefónica* in Spain, and a *télécarte* in France). These are usable only at pay phones, are reasonable for making calls within Spain or within France (and work for international calls as well, though not as cheaply as the international phone cards). Note that insertable phone cards—and most international phone cards—only work in the country where you buy them.

From: rick@ricksteves.com
Sent: Today
To: info@hotelcentral.com
Subject: Reservation request for 19-22 July

Dear Hotel Central,

I would like to reserve a room for 2 people for 3 nights, arriving 19 July and departing 22 July. If possible, I would like a quiet room with a double bed and a bathroom inside the room.

Please let me know if you have a room available and the price.

Thank you!
Rick Steves

Calling from your hotel room phone is usually expensive, unless you use an international phone card. For much more on phoning, see www.ricksteves.com/phoning.

Making Hotel Reservations

To ensure the best value, I recommend reserving rooms in advance, particularly during peak season. Email the hotelier with the following key pieces of information: number and type of rooms; number of nights; date of arrival; date of departure; and any special requests. (For a sample form, see the sidebar.) Use the European style for writing dates: day/month/year. Hoteliers typically ask for your credit-card number as a deposit.

Given the economic downturn, hoteliers may be willing to make a deal—try emailing several hotels to ask their best price. In general, hotel prices can soften if you do any of the following: offer to pay cash, stay at least three nights, or travel off-season.

The French have a simple hotel-rating system based on amenities (from zero through five stars, indicated in this book's French hotel listings by * through *****).

Eating in Spain

By our standards, Spaniards eat late, having lunch—their biggest meal of the day—around 13:00-16:00, and dinner starting about 21:00. At restaurants, you can dine with tourists at 20:00, or with Spaniards if you wait until later.

For a fun early dinner at a bar, build a light meal out of tapas—small appetizer-sized portions of seafood, salads, meat-filled pastries, deep-fried tasties, and so on. Many of these are displayed behind glass, and you can point to what you want. Tapas typically cost about €2-3 apiece, but can run up to €10 for seafood. While the smaller "tapa" size (which comes on a saucer-size plate) is handiest for maximum tasting opportunities, many bars sell only larger sizes: the *ración* (full portion, on a dinner plate) and *media-ración* (half-size portion). *Jamón* (hah-MOHN), an air-dried ham similar to prosciutto, is a Spanish staple. Other key terms include *bocadillo* (baguette sandwich), *frito* (fried), *a la plancha* (grilled), *queso* (cheese), *tortilla* (omelet), and *surtido* (assortment).

Many bars have three price tiers, which should be clearly posted: It's cheapest to eat or drink while standing at the bar (*barra*), slightly more to sit at a table inside (*mesa* or *salón*), and most expensive to sit outside *(terraza)*. Wherever you are, be assertive or you'll never be served. *Por favor* (please) grabs the attention of the server or bartender.

If you're having tapas, don't worry about paying as you go (the bartender keeps track). When you're ready to leave, ask for the bill: *"¿La cuenta?"* To tip for a few tapas, round up to the nearest euro; for a full meal, tip about 5 to 10 percent for good service.

Eating in France

Restaurants serve lunch from about 11:30 to 14:00. They usually open for dinner at 19:00 and are typically most crowded around 20:30. Cafés and brasseries serve throughout the day. They generally have more limited menus than restaurants, but offer more budget options, including salads, sandwiches, omelets, *plats du jour,* and more. Check the price list first, which by law must be posted prominently. There are two sets of prices: You'll pay more for the same drink if you're seated at a table *(salle)* than if you're seated at the bar or counter *(comptoir)*.

In France, an entrée is the first course, and *le plat* or *le plat du jour* is the main course with vegetables. At restaurants, it's common to order *une entrée* and *un plat*, or *un plat* and *un dessert*, or just *un plat*. If you ask for the *menu* (muh-noo), you'll get a fixed-price meal—usually your choice of three courses (soup, appetizer, or salad; main course with vegetables; and cheese course or dessert). Drinks are extra. Ask for *la carte* (lah kart) if you want to see a menu and order à la carte, like the locals do. Request the waiter's help in deciphering the French.

A 12-15 percent service charge *(service compris)* is always included in the bill. Most French never tip, but if you feel the service was exceptional, it's fine to tip up to 5 percent.

Transportation

By Train: To research train schedules, visit Germany's excellent all-Europe website (www.bahn.com), Spain's RENFE (www.renfe.com), or France's SNCF (http://en.voyages-sncf.com).

Long-distance travelers can get a good deal with a Eurail France-Spain pass, sold only outside Europe. For travel only in Spain, RENFE offers their own, eticketed "Renfe Spain Pass." It counts trips instead of calendar days, requires reservations to be made in chronological order, and is only sold on their website. To see if a rail pass could save you money, check www.ricksteves.com/rail.

You can buy tickets at any train station in either country, but remember that in France and Spain, your credit card won't work in payment machines unless it has a chip (go to the ticket window). Many travelers prefer to buy tickets at travel agencies in Spain, because there's less of a language barrier than at the station. In France, you can get tickets at SNCF boutiques—small train offices in the city center. You can purchase tickets online for either country. At the RENFE site, when asked for your Spanish national ID number, enter your passport number—but be aware that the website rejects nearly every attempt to use a US credit card (but it may accept PayPal payments). Since trains can sell out, it's smart to buy tickets at least a day in advance.

In France, you're required to validate (composter, kohm-poh-stay) all train tickets and reservations; before boarding, look for a yellow machine to stamp your ticket or reservation.

By Bus: In Spain and France, buses pick up where the trains don't go, reaching even small villages. In Spain, routes are operated by various competing companies, so it can be tricky to pin down schedules (check with local bus stations, tourist info offices, or www.movelia.es).

By Car: It's cheaper to arrange most car rentals from the US. For tips on your insurance options, see www.ricksteves.com/cdw, and for route planning, consult www.viamichelin.com. Bring your driver's license. In Spain, you're also technically required to have an International Driving Permit (sold at your local AAA office for $15 plus the cost of two passport photos; see www.aaa.com). Superhighways come with tolls, but save lots of time; in France, pay cash at toll booths, since US credit cards won't work unless they have a chip. A car is a worthless headache in cities—park it safely (get tips from your hotel). As break-ins are common, be sure all of your valuables are out of sight and locked in the trunk, or even better, with you or in your hotel room.

Local road etiquette is similar to that in the US. Ask your car-rental company about the rules of the road, or check the US State Department website (www.travel.state.gov, click on "International Travel," then specify your country of choice and click "Traffic Safety and Road Conditions").

By Plane: Consider covering long distances on a budget flight, which can be cheaper than a train ride. To compare several airlines, see www.skyscanner.com. Common budget airlines are easyJet and Ryanair. For flights within Spain, check out www.vueling.com, www.iberia.com, or www.aireuropa.com.

Helpful Hints

Emergency Help in Spain: For police help, dial 091. To summon an ambulance, call 112. For passport problems, call the US Embassy (in Madrid, tel. 915-872-240, http://madrid.usembassy.gov) or the Canadian Embassy (in Madrid, tel. 913-828-400, www.espana.gc.ca).

In either Spain or France, if you have a minor illness, do as the locals do and go to a pharmacist for advice. Or ask at your hotel for help—they know of the nearest medical and emergency services.

Emergency Help in France: In France, dial 112 for any emergency. For English-speaking police help, dial 17. To summon an ambulance (called a "SAMU"), call 15. For passport problems, call the US Consulate and Embassy in Paris (tel. 01 43 12 22 22, http://france.usembassy.gov) or the Canadian Consulate and Embassy in Paris (tel. 01 44 43 29 00, www.france.gc.ca). For other concerns, get advice from your hotelier.

Theft or Loss: Spain and France have particularly hardworking pickpockets—wear a money belt. Assume beggars are pickpockets and any scuffle is simply a distraction by a team of thieves. If you stop for any commotion or show, put your hands in your pockets before someone else does.

To replace a passport, you'll need to go in person to an embassy (see above). Cancel and replace your credit and debit cards by calling these 24-hour US numbers collect: Visa—tel. 303/967-1096, MasterCard—tel. 636/722-7111, American Express—tel. 336/393-1111. In Spain, to make a collect call to the US, dial 900-99-0011; press zero or stay on the line for an operator. In France, dial 0-800-99-0011. File a police report either on the spot or within a day or two; it's required if you submit an insurance claim for lost or stolen rail passes or electronics, and it can help with replacing your passport or credit and debit cards. Precautionary measures can minimize the effects of loss—back up your digital photos and other files frequently. For more information, see www.ricksteves.com/help.

Time: Spain and France use the 24-hour clock. It's the same through 12:00 noon, then keep going: 13:00, 14:00, and so on. Like most of continental Europe, Spain and France are six/nine hours ahead of the East/West Coasts of the US.

Business Hours: In Spain, many shops are generally open Monday-Friday 9:00-13:00 and 16:00-20:00, open Saturday morning, and closed on Sunday. In France, most shops are open Monday-Saturday 10:00–12:00 and 14:00–19:00, closed on Sunday, and in small towns, on Monday mornings as well. In more touristy places in either country, shops can be open throughout the day (without a lunch closure) and on Sunday.

Sights: Major attractions can be swamped with visitors; carefully read and follow this book's crowd-beating tips (visit at quieter times of day, or—where possible—reserve ahead). Opening and closing hours of sights can change unexpectedly; confirm the latest times on their websites or at the local tourist information office. At many churches, a modest dress code is encouraged and sometimes required (no bare shoulders or shorts).

Holidays and Festivals: Spain and France celebrate many holidays, which can close sights and attract crowds (book hotel rooms ahead). For more on holidays and festivals in Spain, check www.spain.info; for France, check http://us.rendezvousenfrance. com. For a simple list showing major—though not all—events, see www.ricksteves.com/festivals.

Numbers and Stumblers: What Americans call the second floor of a building is the first floor in Europe. Europeans write dates as day/month/year, so Christmas is 25/12. Commas are decimal points and vice versa—a dollar and a half is 1,50, and there are 5.280 feet in a mile. Spain and France use the metric system: A kilogram is 2.2 pounds; a liter is about a quart; and a kilometer is six-tenths of a mile.

Resources from Rick Steves

This Snapshot guide is excerpted from *Rick Steves Spain,* which is one of more than 30 titles in my series of guidebooks on European travel. I also produce a public television series, *Rick Steves' Europe,* and a public radio show, *Travel with Rick Steves.* My website, www. ricksteves.com, offers free travel information, a forum for travelers' comments, guidebook updates, my travel blog, an online travel store, and information on European rail passes and our tours of Europe. If you're bringing a mobile device on your trip, you can download free information from Rick Steves Audio Europe, featuring podcasts of my radio shows, free audio tours of major sights in Europe, and travel interviews about Spain and France (via www.ricksteves.com/audioeurope, iTunes, Google Play, or the Rick Steves Audio Europe free smartphone app). You can follow me on Facebook and Twitter.

Additional Resources

Tourist Information: www.spain.info and
http://us.rendezvousenfrance.com
Passports and Red Tape: www.travel.state.gov
Packing List: www.ricksteves.com/packing
Travel Insurance Tips: www.ricksteves.com/insurance
Cheap Flights: www.kayak.com
Airplane Carry-on Restrictions: www.tsa.gov/travelers
Updates for This Book: www.ricksteves.com/update

How Was Your Trip?

If you'd like to share your tips, concerns, and discoveries after using this book, please fill out the survey at www.ricksteves.com/feedback. Thanks in advance—it helps a lot.

Spanish Survival Phrases

Spanish has a guttural sound similar to the J in Baja California. In the phonetics, the symbol for this clearing-your-throat sound is the italicized *h*.

English	Spanish	Pronunciation
Good day.	*Buenos días.*	**bway**-nohs dee-ahs
Do you speak English?	*¿Habla Usted inglés?*	ah-blah oo-**stehd** een-**glays**
Yes. / No.	*Sí. / No.*	see / noh
I (don't) understand.	*(No) comprendo.*	(noh) kohm-**prehn**-doh
Please.	*Por favor.*	por fah-**bor**
Thank you.	*Gracias.*	**grah**-thee-ahs
I'm sorry.	*Lo siento.*	loh see-**ehn**-toh
Excuse me.	*Perdóneme.*	pehr-**doh**-nay-may
(No) problem.	*(No) problema.*	(noh) proh-**blay**-mah
Good.	*Bueno.*	**bway**-noh
Goodbye.	*Adiós.*	ah-dee-**ohs**
one / two	*uno / dos*	**oo**-noh / dohs
three / four	*tres / cuatro*	trays / **kwah**-troh
five / six	*cinco / seis*	**theen**-koh / says
seven / eight	*siete / ocho*	see-**eh**-tay / **oh**-choh
nine / ten	*nueve / diez*	**nway**-bay / dee-**ayth**
How much is it?	*¿Cuánto cuesta?*	**kwahn**-toh **kway**-stah
Write it?	*¿Me lo escribe?*	may loh ay-**skree**-bay
Is it free?	*¿Es gratis?*	ays **grah**-tees
Is it included?	*¿Está incluido?*	ay-**stah** een-kloo-**ee**-doh
Where can I buy / find...?	*¿Dónde puedo comprar / encontrar...?*	**dohn**-day **pway**-doh kohm-**prar** / ayn-kohn-**trar**
I'd like / We'd like...	*Quiero / Queremos...*	kee-**ehr**-oh / kehr-**ay**-mohs
...a room.	*...una habitación.*	**oo**-nah ah-bee-tah-thee-**ohn**
...a ticket to ___.	*...un billete para ___.*	oon bee-**yeh**-tay **pah**-rah ___
Is it possible?	*¿Es posible?*	ays poh-**see**-blay
Where is...?	*¿Dónde está...?*	**dohn**-day ay-**stah**
...the train station	*...la estación de trenes*	lah ay-stah-thee-**ohn** day **tray**-nays
...the bus station	*...la estación de autobuses*	lah ay-stah-thee-**ohn** day ow-toh-**boo**-says
...the tourist information office	*...la oficina de turismo*	lah oh-fee-**thee**-nah day too-**rees**-moh
Where are the toilets?	*¿Dónde están los servicios?*	**dohn**-day ay-**stahn** lohs sehr-**bee**-thee-ohs
men	*hombres, caballeros*	**ohm**-brays, kah-bah-**yay**-rohs
women	*mujeres, damas*	moo-**heh**-rays, **dah**-mahs
left / right	*izquierda / derecha*	eeth-kee-**ehr**-dah / day-**ray**-chah
straight	*derecho*	day-**ray**-choh
When do you open / close?	*¿A qué hora abren / cierran?*	ah kay **oh**-rah **ah**-brehn / thee-**ay**-rahn
At what time?	*¿A qué hora?*	ah kay **oh**-rah
Just a moment.	*Un momento.*	oon moh-**mehn**-toh
now / soon / later	*ahora / pronto / más tarde*	ah-**oh**-rah / **prohn**-toh / mahs **tar**-day
today / tomorrow	*hoy / mañana*	oy / mahn-**yah**-nah

In a Spanish Restaurant

English	Spanish	Pronunciation
I'd like / We'd like...	Quiero / Queremos...	kee-**ehr**-oh / kehr-**ay**-mohs
...to reserve...	...reservar...	ray-sehr-**bar**
...a table for one / two.	...una mesa para uno / dos.	oo-nah may-sah pah-rah oo-noh / dohs
Non-smoking.	No fumador.	noh foo-mah-**dohr**
Is this table free?	¿Está esta mesa libre?	ay-**stah** ay-stah may-sah lee-bray
The menu (in English), please.	La carta (en inglés), por favor.	lah **kar**-tah (ayn een-**glays**) por fah-**bor**
service (not) included	servicio (no) incluido	sehr-**bee**-thee-oh (noh) een-kloo-**ee**-doh
cover charge	precio de entrada	**pray**-thee-oh day ayn-**trah**-dah
to go	para llevar	**pah**-rah yay-**bar**
with / without	con / sin	kohn / seen
and / or	y / o	ee / oh
menu (of the day)	menú (del día)	may-**noo** (dayl **dee**-ah)
specialty of the house	especialidad de la casa	ay-spay-thee-ah-lee-**dahd** day lah **kah**-sah
tourist menu	menú turístico	meh-**noo** too-**ree**-stee-koh
combination plate	plato combinado	**plah**-toh kohm-bee-**nah**-doh
appetizers	tapas	**tah**-pahs
bread	pan	pahn
cheese	queso	**kay**-soh
sandwich	bocadillo	boh-kah-**dee**-yoh
soup	sopa	**soh**-pah
salad	ensalada	ayn-sah-**lah**-dah
meat	carne	**kar**-nay
poultry	aves	**ah**-bays
fish	pescado	pay-**skah**-doh
seafood	marisco	mah-**ree**-skoh
fruit	fruta	**froo**-tah
vegetables	verduras	behr-**doo**-rahs
dessert	postres	**poh**-strays
tap water	agua del grifo	**ah**-gwah dayl **gree**-foh
mineral water	agua mineral	**ah**-gwah mee-nay-**rahl**
milk	leche	**lay**-chay
(orange) juice	zumo (de naranja)	**thoo**-moh (day nah-**rahn**-hah)
coffee	café	kah-**feh**
tea	té	tay
wine	vino	**bee**-noh
red / white	tinto / blanco	**teen**-toh / **blahn**-koh
glass / bottle	vaso / botella	**bah**-soh / boh-**tay**-yah
beer	cerveza	thehr-**bay**-thah
Cheers!	¡Salud!	sah-**lood**
More. / Another.	Más. / Otro.	mahs / **oh**-troh
The same.	El mismo.	ehl **mees**-moh
The bill, please.	La cuenta, por favor.	lah **kwayn**-tah por fah-**bor**
tip	propina	proh-**pee**-nah
Delicious!	¡Delicioso!	day-lee-thee-**oh**-soh

For hundreds more pages of survival phrases for your trip to Spain, check out *Rick Steves' Spanish Phrase Book.*

French Survival Phrases

When using the phonetics, try to nasalize the n̲ sound.

English	French	Pronunciation
Good day.	Bonjour.	bohn̲-zhoor
Mrs. / Mr.	Madame / Monsieur	mah-dahm / muhs-yur
Do you speak English?	Parlez-vous anglais?	par-lay-voo ahn̲-glay
Yes. / No.	Oui. / Non.	wee / nohn̲
I understand.	Je comprends.	zhuh kohn̲-prahn̲
I don't understand.	Je ne comprends pas.	zhuh nuh kohn̲-prahn̲ pah
Please.	S'il vous plaît.	see voo play
Thank you.	Merci.	mehr-see
I'm sorry.	Désolé.	day-zoh-lay
Excuse me.	Pardon.	par-dohn̲
(No) problem.	(Pas de) problème.	(pah duh) proh-blehm
It's good.	C'est bon.	say bohn̲
Goodbye.	Au revoir.	oh vwahr
one / two	un / deux	uhn̲ / duh
three / four	trois / quatre	twah / kah-truh
five / six	cinq / six	san̲k / sees
seven / eight	sept / huit	seht / weet
nine / ten	neuf / dix	nuhf / dees
How much is it?	Combien?	kohn̲-bee-an̲
Write it?	Ecrivez?	ay-kree-vay
Is it free?	C'est gratuit?	say grah-twee
Included?	Inclus?	an̲-klew
Where can I buy / find...?	Où puis-je acheter / trouver...?	oo pwee-zhuh ah-shuh-tay / troo-vay
I'd like / We'd like...	Je voudrais / Nous voudrions...	zhuh voo-dray / noo voo-dree-ohn̲
...a room.	...une chambre.	ewn shahn̲-bruh
...a ticket to ___.	...un billet pour ___.	uhn̲ bee-yay poor
Is it possible?	C'est possible?	say poh-see-bluh
Where is...?	Où est...?	oo ay
...the train station	...la gare	lah gar
...the bus station	...la gare routière	lah gar root-yehr
...tourist information	...l'office du tourisme	loh-fees dew too-reez-muh
Where are the toilets?	Où sont les toilettes?	oo sohn̲ lay twah-leht
men	hommes	ohm
women	dames	dahm
left / right	à gauche / à droite	ah gohsh / ah dwaht
straight	tout droit	too dwah
When does this open / close?	Ça ouvre / ferme à quelle heure?	sah oo-vruh / fehrm ah kehl ur
At what time?	À quelle heure?	ah kehl ur
Just a moment.	Un moment.	uhn̲ moh-mahn̲
now / soon / later	maintenant / bientôt / plus tard	man̲-tuh-nahn̲ / bee-an̲-toh / plew tar

In a French-Speaking Restaurant

English	French	Pronunciation
I'd like / We'd like...	Je voudrais / Nous voudrions...	zhuh voo-dray / noo voo-dree-ohn
...to reserve...	...réserver...	ray-zehr-vay
...a table for one / two.	...une table pour un / deux.	ewn tah-bluh poor uhn / duh
Non-smoking.	Non fumeur.	nohn few-mur
Is this seat free?	C'est libre?	say lee-bruh
The menu (in English), please.	La carte (en anglais), s'il vous plaît.	lah kart (ahn ahn-glay) see voo play
service (not) included	service (non) compris	sehr-vees (nohn) kohn-pree
to go	à emporter	ah ahn-por-tay
with / without	avec / sans	ah-vehk / sahn
and / or	et / ou	ay / oo
special of the day	plat du jour	plah dew zhoor
specialty of the house	spécialité de la maison	spay-see-ah-lee-tay duh lah may-zohn
appetizers	hors-d'oeuvre	or-duh-vruh
first course (soup, salad)	entrée	ahn-tray
main course (meat, fish)	plat principal	plah pran-see-pahl
bread	pain	pan
cheese	fromage	froh-mahzh
sandwich	sandwich	sahnd-weech
soup	soupe	soop
salad	salade	sah-lahd
meat	viande	vee-ahnd
chicken	poulet	poo-lay
fish	poisson	pwah-sohn
seafood	fruits de mer	frwee duh mehr
fruit	fruit	frwee
vegetables	légumes	lay-gewm
dessert	dessert	duh-sehr
mineral water	eau minérale	oh mee-nay-rahl
tap water	l'eau du robinet	loh dew roh-bee-nay
milk	lait	lay
(orange) juice	jus (d'orange)	zhew (doh-rahnzh)
coffee	café	kah-fay
tea	thé	tay
wine	vin	van
red / white	rouge / blanc	roozh / blahn
glass / bottle	verre / bouteille	vehr / boo-teh-ee
beer	bière	bee-ehr
Cheers!	Santé!	sahn-tay
More. / Another.	Plus. / Un autre.	plew / uhn oh-truh
The same.	La même chose.	lah mehm shohz
The bill, please.	L'addition, s'il vous plaît.	lah-dee-see-ohn see voo play
tip	pourboire	poor-bwar
Delicious!	Délicieux!	day-lee-see-uh

For more user-friendly French phrases, check out *Rick Steves' French Phrase Book and Dictionary* or *Rick Steves' French, Italian & German Phrase Book*.

INDEX

Our website enhances this book and turns

Explore Europe

At ricksteves.com you can browse through thousands of articles, videos, photos and radio interviews, plus find a wealth of money-saving travel tips for planning your dream trip. And with our mobile-friendly website, you can easily access all this great travel information anywhere you go.

TV Shows

Preview the places you'll visit by watching entire half-hour episodes of Rick Steves' Europe (choose from all 100 shows) on-demand, for free.

ricksteves.com

your travel dreams into affordable reality

Radio Interviews

Enjoy ready access to Rick's vast library of radio interviews covering travel

tips and cultural insights that relate specifically to your Europe travel plans.

Travel Forums

Learn, ask, share! Our online community of savvy travelers is a great resource

for first-time travelers to Europe, as well as seasoned pros. You'll find forums on each country, plus travel tips and restaurant/hotel reviews. You can even ask one of our well-traveled staff to chime in with an opinion.

Travel News

Subscribe to our free Travel News e-newsletter, and get monthly updates from Rick on what's happening in Europe.

Audio Europe™

Rick's Free Travel App

Get your FREE **Rick Steves Audio Europe**™ app to enjoy…

- Dozens of self-guided tours of Europe's top museums, sights and historic walks

- Hundreds of tracks filled with cultural insights and sightseeing tips from Rick's radio interviews

- All organized into handy geographic playlists

- For iPhone, iPad, iPod Touch, Android

With Rick whispering in your ear, Europe gets even better.

Find out more at ricksteves.com

Rick Steves has

Experience maximum Europe

Save time and energy

This guidebook is your independent-travel toolkit. But for all it delivers, it's still up to you to devote the time and energy it takes to manage the preparation and logistics that are essential for a happy trip. If that's a hassle, there's a solution.

Rick Steves Tours

A Rick Steves tour takes you to Europe's most interesting places with great

great tours, too!

with minimum stress

guides and small groups of 28 or less. We follow Rick's favorite itineraries, ride in comfy buses, stay in family-run hotels, and bring you intimately close to the Europe you've traveled so far to see. Most importantly, we take away the logistical headaches so you can focus on the fun.

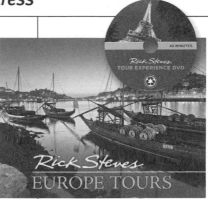

customers—along with us on 40 different itineraries, from Ireland to Italy to Istanbul. Is a Rick Steves tour the right fit for your travel dreams? Find out at ricksteves.com, where you can also get Rick's latest tour catalog and free Tour Experience DVD.

Join the fun

This year we'll take 18,000 free-spirited travelers—nearly half of them repeat

Europe is best experienced with happy travel partners. We hope you can join us.

See our itineraries at ricksteves.com

Rick Steves guidebooks are published by Avalon Travel,
a member of the Perseus Books Group.

NOW AVAILABLE:
eBOOKS, DVD & BLU-RAY

TRAVEL CULTURE

Europe 101
European Christmas
Postcards from Europe
Travel as a Political Act

eBOOKS

Nearly all Rick Steves guides are available as ebooks. Check with your favorite bookseller.

RICK STEVES' EUROPE DVDs

11 New Shows 2013–2014
Austria & the Alps
Eastern Europe
England & Wales
European Christmas
European Travel Skills & Specials
France
Germany, BeNeLux & More
Greece, Turkey & Portugal
Iran
Ireland & Scotland
Italy's Cities
Italy's Countryside
Scandinavia
Spain
Travel Extras

BLU-RAY

Celtic Charms
Eastern Europe Favorites
European Christmas
Italy Through the Back Door
Mediterranean Mosaic
Surprising Cities of Europe

PHRASE BOOKS & DICTIONARIES

French
French, Italian & German
German
Italian
Portuguese
Spanish

JOURNALS

Rick Steves Pocket Travel Journal
Rick Steves Travel Journal

PLANNING MAPS

Britain, Ireland & London
Europe
France & Paris
Germany, Austria & Switzerland
Ireland
Italy
Spain & Portugal

RickSteves.com 🇫 🇾 **@RickSteves**

Rick Steves books and DVDs are available at bookstores and through online booksellers.

Photo © Patricia

Avalon Travel
a member of the Perseus Books Group
1700 Fourth Street
Berkeley, CA 94710

Text © 2014 by Rick Steves' Europe, Inc.

Maps © 2014 by Rick Steves' Europe, Inc. All rights reserved.
Portions of this book originally appeared in *Rick Steves Spain 2015*.

Printed in Canada by Friesens

First printing January 2015

ISBN 978-1-63121-073-0

For the latest on Rick's lectures, guidebooks to many, public radio show and public television
series, contact Rick Steves' Europe, 130 Fourth Avenue North, Edmonds, WA 98020,
425/771-8303, www.ricksteves.com, rick@ricksteves.com.

Rick Steves' Europe
Managing Editor: Risa Laib
Editorial & Production Manager: Jennifer Madison Davis
Editors: Glenn Eriksen, Tom Griffin, Cameron Hewitt, Suzanne Kotz, Cathy Lu,
  John Pierce, Carrie Shepherd
Editorial & Production Assistant: Jessica Shaw
Editorial Intern: Mallory Presho-Dunne
Researchers: Amanda Buttinger, Trish Feaster, Suzanne Kotz
Maps & Graphics: David C. Hoerlein, Sandra Hundacker, Lauren Mills, Mary Rostad

Avalon Travel
Senior Editor and Series Manager: Madhu Prasher
Editor: Jamie Andrade
Associate Editor: Maggie Ryan
Copy Editor: Suzie Nasol
Proofreader: Rebecca Freed
Indexer: Stephen Callahan
Production & Typesetting: McGuire Barber Design
Cover Design: Kimberly Glyder Design
Maps & Graphics: Kat Bennett, Mike Morgenfeld, Lohnes + Wright

Photo Credits
Front Cover: Bay of La Concha, San Sebastián, Spain © 123rf.com
Title Page Photo: Peine de los Vientos, Chillida rusty steel sculpture in San Sebastián
  © 123rf.com
Page 1 Photo: view of the Cathedral of Good Shepherd in San Sebastián © 123rf.com
Additional Photography: Dominic Bonuccelli, Cameron Hewitt, David C. Hoerlein,
  Suzanne Kotz, Cathy McDonald, Pat O'Connor, Gene Openshaw, Rick Steves, Robert
  Wright, Wikimedia Commons (PD-Art/PD-US). Photos are used by permission and
  are the property of the original copyright owners.

ABOUT THE AUTHOR

RICK STEVES

Since 1973, Rick Steves has spent 100 days every year exploring Europe. Along with writing and researching a bestselling series of guidebooks, Rick produces a public television series *(Rick Steves' Europe)*, a public radio show *(Travel with Rick Steves)*, a blog (on Facebook), and an app and podcast *(Rick Steves Audio Europe)*; writes a nationally syndicated newspaper column; organizes guided tours that take over 15,000 travelers to Europe annually; and offers an information-packed website (www.ricksteves.com). With the help of his hardworking staff of 90 at Rick Steves' Europe—in Edmonds, Washington, just north of Seattle—Rick's mission is to make European travel fun, affordable, and culturally enlightening for Americans.

Connect with Rick:

facebook.com/RickSteves   twitter: @RickSteves